Collaborative
SELLING

Collaborative
SELLING
HOW TO GAIN THE
COMPETITIVE ADVANTAGE IN SALES

Dr. Tony Alessandra
Rick Barrera, CSP

John Wiley & Sons, Inc.
New York • Chichester • Brisbane • Toronto • Singapore

Copyright © 1993 by Dr. Tony Alessandra and Rick Barrera, CSP
Published by John Wiley & Sons, Inc.

Library of Congress Cataloging-in-Publication Data

Alessandra, Tony
    Collaborative selling : how to gain the competitive advantage in
  sales / Tony Alessandra and Rick Barrera.
        p.   cm.
    Based on the author's audio program The edge, released by
  Dartnell.
    Includes index.
    ISBN 0-471-59664-7 (cloth). — ISBN 0-471-59665-5 (paper)
    1. Selling. 2. Sales personnel. I. Barrera, Rick. II. Title.
  HF5438.25.A42   1993
  658.85—dc20   93-13175

Printed in the United States of America
10 9 8 7 6 5 4 3

To Holli Olson Catchpole,
my Vice President of Sales & Marketing,
who is the epitome of a collaborative salesperson.
—T.A.

To my fiancée and lifelong love, Keely.
—R.B.

About the Authors

Dr. Tony Alessandra

Dr. Tony Alessandra is one of the top sales and communications keynote speakers in the United States. For the past 17 years, Alessandra has given an average of 100 speeches per year and in 1985, he received the prestigious C.P.A.E. (Council of Peers Award for Excellence) from the National Speakers Association. This award, given in recognition of speaking excellence, is bestowed upon only five recipients per year.

He brings to the speaker's platform years of practical sales experience combined with a solid educational background. He grew up in New York City and worked his way through college selling door-to-door, winning numerous awards. He received his Bachelors in Business Administration, Masters of Business Administration, and Ph.D. in Marketing from Notre Dame, the University of Connecticut, and Georgia State University respectively. He taught sales and marketing at the university level from 1970–1978.

Alessandra has written nearly 50 articles and has syndicated them more than 500 times in over 100 professional and trade journals. He has also co-authored eleven books, including the popular *Non-Manipulative Selling* and *The Art of Managing People.*

Rick Barrera

Rick Barrera is a certified speaker, sales trainer, and consultant based in La Jolla, California. He delivers seminars and programs that are designed to initiate and produce shifts in the organizational culture for many Fortune 500 corporations and professional associations. Rick brings to his work experience from an award-winning 15-year sales career that included telemarketing, door-to-door, business-to-business, wholesale and retail selling, sales management, marketing, and advertising.

Traveling worldwide over 150 days a year, Rick Barrera has delivered hundreds of programs on *Collaborative Selling, Peak Performance,* and *Customer Service* to a select clientele, including AT&T, Xerox, IBM Corporation, Intel, Johnson Controls, Blue Cross Blue Shield, Tupperware International, Gannet Media, and Glamour Magazine.

Rick is co-author of the business best-seller *Non-Manipulative Selling,* the comprehensive audio & video sales training series *The Competitive Advantage,* and most recently *The Edge—How to Gain a Competitive Advantage in Selling* audio program published by Dartnell. All of his programs are based on a sound philosophy and an art for fine-tuning the sales, management, and marketing practices that drive a company. To his clients he brings a fresh, dynamic approach, solid information, and guaranteed systems for successful implementation.

Acknowledgments

We would like to thank the people without whom this book would not have been possible. Thanks to Joyce Wycoff for adding her input, insights, and polish to the manuscript; to Cindy Spring for refining the script for the audio program, *The Edge*, released by Dartnell, on which this book is based; and to the following individuals whose assistance in developing the initial concept for the video training series, *The Competitive Advantage*, contributed greatly to this work. Thank you to Sue Alessandra, Gary Alessandra, Gregg Baron, Doug Breekner, Holli Catchpole, Robert Coates, Mike Davis, Curt Ittner, Dee Jones, Adelina Liwag, Keely Smith, Rob Sommer, and Peter Wheeler.

A Note on the Personal Pronoun

To avoid sexism without resorting to such awkward and tedious compounds and combinations as *he/she, his or hers,* and so on, we have used the masculine and feminine pronouns arbitrarily throughout this book. For example, the phrase "help your client solve his problems" might just as easily have been written with "her."

Contents

Introduction

The world has changed in significant ways, and salespeople today must have new skills, new attitudes, and a new understanding of how to work with their clients.

Here are a few questions that might help demonstrate this point:

- Have you found that your competitors are more *aggressive* than they used to be?
- Do you have *more* competitors than you've had in the past?
- Does it seem harder to *sell* your product now than it was just a few years ago?
- Are you finding it harder to *differentiate* yourself from your competitors?
- Are *price issues* a constant problem?

If you answered "yes" to more than one of these questions, it's because your company is participating in a worldwide quantum shift that's particularly acute in the United States. There are three key aspects to this shift:

Technology   For most products, technology is no longer a differentiator. Most of your competitors have about the same technology as you do, which means your products have about the same features. In the past, it was possible to have a technical breakthrough that would give you years of competitive advantage. Only a few companies can claim today that their product is radically different from that of the competition . . . and that difference generally lasts only a few months or years at most.

Global market   We're selling in a *global* marketplace, which means we have more and different competitors than we've had in the past. The arrival of new competitors has also created more confusion in the marketplace—not only for us but for our customers.

Supply exceeds demand   For most businesses, more products and services are available than the market as a whole wants to buy. In the past, businesses with quality products were reasonably sure they would be able to sell them. Today, that may no longer be true. Do you remember "the good old days" of 1983 when the phone company was still a monopoly and connecting new service could take weeks? Today, you have literally dozens of choices and it takes only minutes to connect you!

What all this means is that buyers today are overwhelmed by more choices of products and suppliers than they could ever possibly use. If you want to be successful in today's market, you must be able to get the buyer's attention, and to do that you must be able to *differentiate* yourself, your company, and your product.

In the '80s you had to do more with less. Today you have to do more with less *and* do it faster. Quality that you can document is essential to survive in today's market, and exceptional customer service delivered by your company—and *you*—is more important than ever.

Today's customers aren't looking for quick fixes, either. They're looking for long-term relationships with suppliers who'll be resources for them over the long haul. *Your ability to collaborate and partner with your customers will make or break your career.* Your sales success in the information age will depend on your ability to learn about and adapt to the realities of a new and very different marketplace.

Another reason the selling systems of the past won't work today is because they were designed to work in a different environment . . . an adversarial one. Today, many companies award lifetime contracts to their supplier-partners. Companies network their computer systems together for order entry, just-in-time inventory control, and electronic payment. When your customers are your partners—and you want them as *lifetime* partners—you can't sell using commando tactics. An adversarial relationship just won't work.

Selling effectively today means handling all the interpersonal aspects of a sale better than you have in the past, and that's what this book is designed to help you do. We'll show you how to excel in this tougher, faster, more complex selling arena. When you really understand the tools and information in this book, you'll find that you'll win more sales, do it in less time, and build a strong base of lifelong customers who will act as both references *and* sources of referrals. We'll show you how to identify your target accounts, how to sell to them without manipulation, and how to penetrate each account to maximize its potential.

Whether you're a newcomer or a seasoned professional, you'll find ideas in this book that will take your *selling skills* and your *sales* to new levels. As you put these ideas into practice, you'll see your success with customers soar right along with your commissions. As these skills become second nature to you, you'll soon see yourself as a cutting-edge sales professional who knows what it takes to win in the information age. In a short time you'll find that you truly have discovered the advantages of *Collaborative Selling*.

What's Wrong with Traditional Selling?

Throughout this book we'll be discussing the differences between our collaborative approach to selling and the traditional approach. Let us explain what we mean by traditional. The traditional approach to selling developed largely during the years following World War II. When the war ended, demand for consumer goods was at an all-time high, and consumers were not as sophisticated as they are today. Selling involved razzle-dazzle pitches that highlighted a product's new technical features followed by a strong close that would let the buyer know that this was his last chance to buy the product or it would be offered to someone else. The traditional salesperson needed the ability to overcome all of the buyer's objections immediately because he had to move on to the next prospect. It was strictly a one-shot deal.

Today's customers buy differently. They know there's no real urgency because the good deal will still be there tomorrow or it may be replaced by a better one. Today's customers have learned to shop around, and they know they have lots of very similar options from other vendors. They're looking for measurable quality in what they buy and for a company and a salesperson who will be there when they need help. In other words, they're not just looking to buy a product, they're looking for a long-term relationship with their supplier. Terms like strategic alliance, sustaining resource, single source, integrity, values, and ethics are increasingly being used to describe the current nature of the buyer/seller relationship.

The traditional salesperson paid very little attention to targeting specific markets and planning sales calls. The plan was to deliver the same pitch with little variation to as many people as possible, in the least amount of time. A salesperson who contacted a prospect spent a few minutes engaging in small talk to break the ice, asked a few fact-finding questions, then launched right into the presentation with very little knowledge of the customer's true needs. The pitch had to cover all of the product's features and benefits because the salesperson couldn't be sure which ones would be relevant to the prospect. Then came the close. What do you think happened?

Let's review this by putting you in the role of the customer. A salesperson contacts you, asks you a couple of questions, delivers a presentation on a product that may have little to do with your needs, and then asks you if you'd like to buy some. If you're an intelligent, reasonably assertive person, what would you say? "No!" Of course! But the salesperson expects that. Everyone says no at first! So she asks you, "Why not?" and the objection game begins. Can you think up more objections than she can overcome? If so, you win! If not, you lose! Now, think about that process: hard sales pitch unrelated to customer needs . . . manipulative closing tactics . . . high-pressure attempts to overcome objections . . . and if you buy, the salesperson is gone, on to the next target. Is this the basis for a long-term relationship?

How many referrals would you be willing to provide after an adversarial sales process like that? How willing would you be to repeat the process in the future? And if you have a problem with the product, what would your attitude be? Would you be committed to making the product work out or would you be more inclined to be looking for flaws? And how much follow-up would you expect from this salesperson? None, probably . . . unless she wants to sell you something else!

What's missing in traditional selling is the salesperson's commitment to a long-term relationship. Short-term thinking creates an adversarial environment, and in an adversarial environment everyone loses. This whole process creates negative tension for both the buyer and the seller. Neither party is comfortable; but successful, traditional salespeople learn to live with the tension, and customers learn how to avoid getting into these situations in the first place. If you want to see traditional selling in its classic form, just go to your local car dealer. Most haven't changed their sales process since the '50s. They still think short-term and can't understand why people avoid buying new cars!

In a long-term relationship, you're more concerned about quality than your customers are, because it supports *their* customers' purchases, which in turn affect their future orders from you. Your customers are more concerned with your profitability because they want you to be a viable supply source when it comes time to reorder.

Why Collaborative Selling Works Better

It doesn't take a genius to figure out that the emphasis in traditional selling is in the wrong place. *The collaborative salesperson takes the time up front to build a sincere, committed relationship and to learn in-depth about the customer's needs.* This makes the entire sales process a positive experience, and it ensures that the environment will be cooperative rather than adversarial. Six key words describe how the collaborative sales process unfolds: *targeting, contacting, exploring, collaborating, confirming,* and *assuring.* Let's take an overview of the process:

Targeting your market   This step helps you understand exactly what you have to offer that's unique and exactly which *target* audiences can best use what you have to sell. It takes some time, but your success ratios will be much higher because you'll be focusing your efforts only on those prospects who have a high probability of buying. Then you'll work to see that these prospects have a positive image of you *before* you call on them.

Contacting your prospect   When you do contact your prospect, you'll be prepared to convey your *advantages*, your *credibility*, and your *sincere desire* to be of service. You'll develop trust and gather a complete picture of their situation, their needs, and their opportunities before you talk at all about your product or service. You'll let your prospect know you're there to help more than you're there to sell.

Exploring your customer's needs   Rather than delivering a pitch, you'll explore options with your client to develop solutions that you feel might work in his situation.

Collaborating with your customer   Together you'll select the options that look like the best fit. Your client will have as much as or more input into the creation and the selection of options than you do. This process ensures that he will be as committed to implementing the solution as you are. After all, why would he invest his time in creating a solution he's not committed to buy?

Confirming the sale   This step is the logical conclusion to the continual communication and problem-solving process you've been in with your client. You're not ending the process, you're beginning it. Confirmation becomes a question of when, not if. If the client does resist, it simply indicates a need to gather more information or clarify some details. When your prospect has helped co-design the solution and "buys in," then you don't need to "close" him. If he feels his needs are being met, he'll buy!

Assuring customer satisfaction   The final step begins immediately after the sale. You change hats from "salesperson" to "quality-control person." You'll help your customers track their results and analyze the effectiveness of your solution. By assuring their satisfaction, you'll build a large, loyal clientele that will guarantee future sales and referrals.

Sounds pretty good, doesn't it? If you're like most salespeople, you're probably saying, "I sell like that already. I'm not a traditional salesperson." That's great! It probably means that you lean more toward collaborative than traditional, but you may still have some traditional tools in your sales kit. You're most likely doing what we call quasi-traditional selling. Quasi-traditional selling is where you embrace the *philosophy* of collaborative selling, but you continue to use some of the skills and techniques of traditional selling. If you still have negative tension in the sales process, or find yourself in an adversarial environment, or close hard to get the sale, or have a lot of price resistance, or find yourself handling a lot of objections, there's still some quasi-traditional selling going on.

If you're still not sure whether you may be practicing quasi-traditional selling, try this quick quiz:

1. Do you think in terms of orders or relationships?
2. Do you try to win versus trying to help?
3. Do you make presentations or do you involve and facilitate?
4. Do you try to impose solutions or elicit solutions?
5. Do you avoid or ignore issues or do you work to solve issues?
6. Do you try to negotiate for top dollar or look out for the best long-term interests of your customer?
7. When there's a problem, do you find yourself protecting your company or your customer?
8. Do you make the sale and move on or measure outcomes and assure satisfaction?
9. Do you generally get one order per customer or do you fully leverage your sales activities through referrals and expansion within the customer's environment?
10. Do you see yourself as a supplier or as an integrated partner?

If you selected the first option in any of the preceding questions, you're practicing quasi-traditional selling. You may be embracing the philosophy of collaborative selling, but from your client's viewpoint, it still looks like traditional selling.

Throughout this book, you'll be learning all of the specific skills and techniques you'll need to effectively practice collaborative selling, so your clients will see you as a partner rather than an adversary. This will enable you to become even more of a superstar than you are now, and you'll find that selling will be even more fun as you put these techniques into practice.

If you're new to the sales profession, you'll learn the correct way to sell right from the beginning. If you're an old pro, you'll have an opportunity to refine your skills, be reminded of some things you may have forgotten, and learn some new skills along the way.

As you read *Collaborative Selling*, picture yourself applying these ideas; hear yourself saying the words that will help you to explore, collaborate, confirm, and assure your client. Feel yourself being a friend and a partner to that person, not an adversary. Remember that the emphasis here is not so much on *what* you sell, but *who* you are in the selling situation.

STEP I

Targeting Your Market

The targeting step of sales includes three phases:

1. Understanding and being able to state your competitive advantages.
2. Identifying and finding your best prospects.
3. Using personal marketing techniques to generate leads.

Targeting helps you understand exactly what you have to offer that's unique, and exactly which target audiences can best use what you have to sell. Until you understand what makes your product or service different from that of the competition, you really don't know what benefits you have to offer your customer. And, until you can state your competitive advantage in a short, simple statement, your prospects will not understand what you have to offer.

Once you understand your competitive advantage, it is important to identify the prospects who will have the highest need for your product or service. These are your best prospects . . . the ones who are most likely to buy, use, and recommend you and your services.

When you have identified your best prospects and know where to find them, you can use your personal marketing skills to generate leads that will most likely result in sales. These techniques can actually help you create an environment where your prospects call you! Lead generation is the fuel that drives the engine of your sales success. The techniques discussed in this chapter can keep you supplied with highly qualified leads for the remainder of your sales career.

Targeting allows you to focus your efforts on those prospects who are most likely to buy from you. Then you'll work on powerful visibility strategies to see that these prospects have a positive image of you *before* you contact them. When you do call them, you'll quickly be able to give them a powerful statement of your competitive advantage.

CHAPTER 1

Demonstrate Your Competitive Advantage

As we've traveled around the country over the past several years working with salespeople, we've been amazed to find that they do not know and cannot articulate their competitive advantages. How can a salesperson expect prospects and customers to give their time and attention if they do not understand, clearly and concisely, what that salesperson can do for them that no one else can do? The inability to differentiate yourself is what we call "selling in the pit."

Salespeople who don't understand their competitive advantage are all in a deep pit saying things like, "Our product is better quality," or "Our service is better," or "I'm my company's competitive advantage." Even if you are your company's competitive advantage, you won't convince your customers just by saying so, because many of your competitors will be saying the same thing! To get out of the pit, you have to *define* quality. You have to *show* the prospect what outstanding service looks like and *how your service differs from that of the competition.*

In a moment we'll show you how to determine your competitive advantage. But first let's talk about how you can demonstrate your competitive advantage from the very moment you are introduced. Suppose someone walks up to you at a business conference, introduces herself, and asks you what you do for a living. *Exactly* what would you say?

Did you have any trouble coming up with a response? Did you stumble? Do you know what sets you apart from your competitors? If this was hard for you, you're not alone. If you were to ask the average car, computer, or caviar salesperson what they do for a living, they'll probably say, "I sell cars, computers, or caviar." And what does every other car, computer, or caviar salesperson say? Exactly the same thing!

Declaring Your Competitive Advantage

So what *should* the salesperson who understands his competitive advantage say? How about this for the car salesperson:

"My name is Mike and I work with Competitive Motors. We've found that there is a lot of confusion in the automotive market today because there have been over 150 new models introduced in just the past three years. I've developed a computer program that profiles everything the buyer wants in a car, and in less than five minutes, identifies the models most likely to fit his or her needs."

Mike has given his prospect a *statement of competitive advantage*, a 30-second statement of what differentiates *you* in the marketplace. It has four components:

1. Your name.
2. Your company.
3. A statement about a problem in your market.
4. How you and your product solve that problem.

Here's another example:

"My name is Marlene and I work with a company called 'The Prescription for Doctors.' Physicians today are being pressured by insurers, employers, and patients to cut health care costs. Yet overhead costs for physicians are constantly rising. We provide a service that allows the physician to spend more time with patients and cut overhead costs at the same time, resulting in better-quality care at a lower cost. It's just what the doctor ordered!"

Here's one last example:

"My name is Beth. I'm with a company called 'The Greatest Advertising Agency in the World.' We've discovered that almost every successful product either has been the first entry in its category or has been able to create a new category in the mind of its customers. What we do is help companies who are launching new products or having trouble with old ones ensure that their product is positioned to win!"

A statement of competitive advantage really does set you apart from the competition. And it makes you sound like a polished expert right from the start. Worksheet 1.1 will help you determine *your* competitive advantage statement.

Determining Your Competitive Advantage

But how do *you* determine exactly what *your* competitive advantage is? The best way is to break down the components of your product or service into four distinct categories:

WORKSHEET 1.1

Your Competitive Advantage Statement

Develop a competitive advantage statement for your *primary* target market:

Target market 1 _____

Your name _____

Your company _____

■ What is a typical problem experienced in this target market? ____

_____

_____

■ What's an intriguing statement about how you and your product solve this problem? _____

_____

_____

_____

Develop another competitive advantage statement for another prime target market:

Target market 2 _____

Your name _____

Your company _____

■ What is a typical problem experienced in this target market? ____

_____

_____

_____

■ What's an intriguing statement about how you and your product solve this problem? _____

_____

_____

_____

Competitive uniqueness   Ask yourself, "What can I do for my customers that no one else can do? What can I offer that no one else can?" For example, suppose a pharmaceutical company receives FDA approval to sell a new drug. Since no one else has the drug, this company now has a competitive uniqueness with this drug.

Competitive advantage   Ask yourself, "What can I do for my customers that my competitor can also do, but I can do it better and I can prove it?" For example, suppose two companies market the same drug, but one is a large, well-known company and the other is a small, relatively unknown company. Even though both are selling essentially the same product, the larger company has an advantage because it's well known, and people ask for the drug by its company name because of its wide recognition. If no real competitive advantage exists in your product, try to focus on your company reputation, your excellent service, your responsiveness and reliability, or any other factors that can positively differentiate you from your competition.

Competitive parity   Here, you are saying, "Objectively speaking, my competitors and I are the same here—there is no real differentiation." Ask yourself what things are the same between you and the competition? What do you have that is exactly like what the competition offers and is important to the customer? Birth control pills are a good example. Several ethical drug companies make different formulations, but they all have similar records for preventing pregnancy. This is competitive parity.

Competitive disadvantages   Honestly answer the question, "Where does the competition have an advantage over me?" What specific disadvantages does your product or service possess? What does the competition do better than you do? Your drug may have more side effects than the competitor's. That's a competitive disadvantage.

You may want to do your analysis by market segment, competitor, or by product or include all these factors, but knowing your competitive position will quickly get you out of the pit and on your customer's wavelength.

In the examples we've just given, we talked about the whole product as either unique or the same as a competitor's. But what do you do if some features of your product are unique, some are advantages, some are the same, and some are disadvantages? Say, for example, that you are selling a fax machine that uses plain paper. That's *parity*, because others do, too.

But maybe yours is the only one that will interface with telephones, computers, or car phones. That's *uniqueness*. Yours also has the highest resolution available—that's an *advantage*. Yours has a 300-number memory, compared to their 200-number memory, another *advantage*, but it will not do broadcasting and polling—that's a *disadvantage*.

Here's an example in a service business. Federal Express will deliver your package overnight (but so will other companies; that's parity), by 10:30 A.M. (which used to be an advantage, but now others are doing it, so it has become parity). But Federal Express has a documented better track record than its competitors—an advantage—and they can tell you at any time exactly where your package is; that's uniqueness. (Of course, in the rapidly changing world of service businesses, some of these benefits may have changed from advantages to parity, or vice versa, by the time you read this.)

We can't stress enough the importance of analyzing your competitive advantage (see Worksheet 1.2). By doing this analysis you'll be in a position to help your customers differentiate you from your competitors. Once they see your uniquenesses and advantages, it will be easier for them to make a decision in your favor.

To discover your competitive advantage, you may have to do some intelligence gathering—talk to your customers and other salespeople, read the local newspapers, attend trade shows, talk to your customers' suppliers, assemble a file of your competitors' marketing and product information, analyze why you lose customers to competitors, use a clipping service to gather information on competitors or on major prospects, obtain annual and quarterly reports of your competitors and prospective customers, watch the market trends in your industry and in your customers' industries—in other words, become the expert on your product or service and how it can help your customers. Complete Worksheet 1.2 to determine your competitive uniqueness, advantages, parities, and disadvantages versus those of two of your major competitors.

Warning: Don't focus on price as a competitive advantage   How many times have you been in a selling situation where the customer's sole focus was price? Any time your customers *can't tell the difference* between your product or service and your competitor's, they will buy on price.

You must differentiate your company, your product, your quality, your service, and yourself if you want the customer to stop focusing on price and start seeing you as a partner, not just as a supplier. You've got to show your customer *how* you are different.

WORKSHEET 1.2
Competitive Analysis

Complete the following chart to determine your competitive strengths and weaknesses versus those of two of your major competitors.

Competitive Factors	Versus Competitor A	Versus Competitor B
Uniqueness What do I have that the competition doesn't have?		
Advantages What do I have that the competition also has, but ours is better?		
Parity What do I have that is the same as the competition's but is still important to the customer?		
Disadvantages What does the competition have that I don't?		

How to Use Your Competitive Advantages to Increase Sales

I'm sure you can see now why it's so important to know what you have to offer that's unique. But you may be wondering what you'll do with that information once you have it. How will you get it across to the client? You're going to use this information in every step of the sale. Your entire sales effort will be built around your competitive strengths:

- *When you are targeting your market,* you'll be looking for those clients whose needs are most likely to match your uniquenesses and advantages.
- *When you contact clients,* you'll open the conversation by letting them know what you can do for them that no one else can do.
- *During the exploring phase,* you'll be asking questions that will uncover client needs in the areas where you have uniquenesses and advantages.
- *When you are collaborating with your client,* you'll keep him focused on your uniquenesses and advantages and show him how they match his needs.
- *During the confirming phase,* you'll be summarizing all of the competitive advantages that your product has to offer.
- *During the assuring phase,* you'll be measuring how well your uniquenesses and advantages are serving your customer.

Summing Up

Let's summarize the powerful strategies we've talked about so far that will give you a competitive advantage. First, know what your competitive advantages and uniquenesses are, and second, be able to articulate them clearly to prospective customers in 30 seconds or less, in your statement of competitive advantage. This is your powerful opening to your targeted prospects, that all-important first impression that sets you apart from your competition. The next chapter will help you identify and target the prospects who are most likely to need your particular competitive advantage.

CHAPTER 2

Identifying and Finding Your Best Customers

Now that you know how to identify and state your competitive advantage, how can you identify those customers who are most likely to want to hear your message? And once you've identified the profile of those most likely to buy, where can you find large numbers of customers who fit that profile?

Unless you are just starting in sales, look to your existing customer base for clues. Your current customers can point the way to others who might purchase in the future, because you'll probably find that your existing customers and your best potential customers have similar demographic and psychographic profiles. By *demographic* we mean that they have similar incomes, occupations, or educational levels; are in the same industries; have similar structures or distribution systems; hold the same position within the company; and so on. By *psychographic* we mean that they share similar beliefs, attitudes, values, priorities, and buying patterns.

Here's a good example of how you might use demographic profiling of your existing customers to help you find new customers:

> Suppose a review of your most profitable accounts shows that you've had success in the past selling your computer system to multibranch banks. It would make sense to keep calling on multibranch banks and to place a higher priority on them than you would on, say, hardware stores where you've never sold a system. You might build on that success by calling on organizations that have a similar structure in similar industries, such as multibranch consumer-lending companies.
>
> If you were to ask those banks specifically *why* they bought from you and they responded by saying that they felt comfortable with you because of your reputation for 24-hour support, your error-free software, and your one-year money-back guarantee, you would have the beginnings of some psychographic data—in other words, a profile of your customers' *buying values*. To refine it a bit more, you might ask them to reduce their reason for buying to one word or one sentence. In this case they might say "reliability and peace of mind." When

approaching other banks and consumer-lending companies, you would then use reliability and peace of mind as your focus for talking about your competitive advantage and point to your reputation for 24-hour support, error-free software, and one-year money-back guarantee as evidence of your claim of reliability and peace of mind.

How to Identify Your *Best* Customers

Don't just guess or assume. Look at your demographic and psychographic data. You may be surprised to find out that the customers you regard as major accounts aren't necessarily the volume leaders; high visibility doesn't always translate into high volume. And often you'll find that the high-volume accounts aren't necessarily the high-profit accounts. They may be discounted deeply or require more servicing than some smaller accounts. So your current *best* customers *may not be your current biggest customers.* How do you identify your best customers?

Your study should begin with an analysis of your sales over the last two to three years. If you are new to sales or to your company, look to experienced salespeople or to your sales managers for help here. In your analysis, you'll look for three things:

1. Who bought what?
2. Exactly how did you find and sell those customers?
3. Why did they buy what they bought?

Look at Who Bought What

Which customers accounted for your past sales? What products or services did they buy and how much did they buy? Which sales were the most profitable? Which ones had the shortest sales cycles? Take a close look at which industry and segment of the market these accounts are in. The United States Chamber of Commerce has a coding system for every industry group and subgroup. These are called Standard Industrial Classifications or SIC codes. Identify the SIC codes of your best customers. The reference librarian at your local library can help you. Your goal is to identify the patterns in your high-volume and high-profit customers—the ones who provided *the most valuable business* to your company.

It's sometimes strategically valuable to sell to a customer who might not provide you a high profit but is high in prestige. Sometimes a company wants an industry leader on its customer list because of their prominence in a given industry. The fact that the leader has selected *you* can influence others to do business with you as well.

Some companies want to build market share regardless of volume and profit. If your company's primary focus is on building market share, you'll want to target *all* the possible customers who could buy your product. Whichever factors you use, determine the profile of your company's best customers: *Who bought what?*

How Did You Find and Sell Those Customers?

Next, look at the *sources* of your best customers. Exactly *how* was that business acquired? Where did the initial contact come from? Was it a referral, a cold call, a walk-in, or a trade show lead, or was it in response to an ad or a trade journal article you wrote? Who handled it initially and who finally brought in the business?

Look for *patterns*! Find out what you are doing that is working. Success leaves clues, so look for them. This will help you focus on your highest-leverage opportunities for reaching similar customers. If you can find a pattern in your existing customer profiles, you should be able to find new customers who are likely to buy by finding other companies that fit the pattern of your existing customers.

After you've got a good profile of what your best customers look like and you've discovered the patterns that have brought you together successfully in the past, ask yourself where you can find lots more customers that fit your profile. Here are some potential sources:

Industry associations   For business-to-business selling, you should always start with industry associations. Just about every industry group in this country that you can imagine has an association. Your local reference librarian can help you find them, or you may want to check with the American Society of Association Executives (ASAE). Often associations are listed in the local telephone directory, or you may want to look in the directory for your state capital or in Washington, D.C., for statewide and national associations. Because most of them have a state or national lobbying arm, you'll find they tend to cluster around government centers. You may also want to check out New York City or Chicago since many are headquartered there. Your local phone company can get you directories for any city.

Mailing lists   Your local phone book also lists mailing-list brokers who can provide you with lists of companies by industry or SIC code, and they can often provide phone numbers and key contacts as well. For person-to-person selling, directories are available that list professionals, small business owners, affluent individuals, and so on. Other sources include list brokers, magazine subscribers, and catalog mailing lists or customer lists from other companies.

Previous clients   Don't forget to consider past clients who may not be current clients.

U.S. Census information   Be sure to check with the U.S. Census Bureau. Data from the 1990 census are now available in some very sophisticated yet usable formats. If you have a good customer demographic profile, the census data can pinpoint your customers right to a given street or neighborhood.

Civic and professional groups   If you're working with a local target market, you might look at which civic or professional groups your customers belong to. Some groups, such as the Rotary Club or an association of professional businesswomen, may rent out their membership lists whereas others will require you to join to get it.

Customers who buy products related to your product   Take a look at what other related products your best customers might buy in conjunction with your products, such as software and hardware, printing and graphic design services, or office furniture and carpeting. Is it possible for you to do a joint promotion or to exchange lists with a noncompetitor who also sells to your target market?

Trade journals   What trade journals do your best customers read? If you can write an article for one of your industry trade journals, you can establish yourself as an expert in your area. Publishing articles is an excellent way to increase your visibility in your target markets.

The questions you want to answer are these: Where do people with the demographics or psychographics that are the same as those of my best customers cluster? Where can I find large groups of them in one place?

Why Did They Buy What They Bought?

What exactly is it about your product, service, or company that makes it attractive to your best customers? Why are they buying from you and not your competitors? Perhaps it's because others they trust know you and buy from you. They may buy because of physical proximity. They may buy because your credit terms are favorable. Sometimes you'll find that it's just habit or that they are unaware of other suppliers. You'll need to ask to find out.

Identify Which Person in the Company Is the Decision Maker

There's one more common denominator to look for in this analysis when you're selling to the business market. With which contacts in the customers' organizations have you had the most success? What position within the company do most of your first contacts and ultimate buyers hold? Is it the president, vice president of marketing, director of operations, director of management information systems, purchasing manager, or someone else? Identifying these key contacts will let you know to whom you should direct your selling efforts.

Every company is different. Sometimes it does make sense to go to the person most likely to *buy* your product, such as the purchasing department. But more often, it makes more sense to go to the highest-level person in the company who recognizes the problem your product or service solves. In a small company, that might mean calling on the president or CEO. In a larger company, that might mean contacting someone at the executive level—a director or vice president. Keep in mind that in the selling process you'll need to meet the needs of gatekeepers, users, buyers, influencers, and deciders, but ultimately it's the decider who needs to say yes. Starting too low in the organization could be the kiss of death. The president or department head may not be the one who places the order with you, but she can provide valuable information on the company and can tell you who you need to see to get action. Besides, what better way to get in to see the purchasing manager than to say you were referred by the president?

Using Information About Your Best Customers to Find *New* Customers

Whatever you find out is valuable information because it tells you how you can best represent your products and services to prospective customers, and it will give you some insights into the ways your customers see you, your company, and your products.

By now, you should have a clear picture of what types of buying preferences typify your best customers. This, then, allows you to identify prospects who fit that best-customer profile. Using the criteria set forth in your analysis, you can identify potential buyers who are likely to have the same needs and might buy for the same reasons as your best current accounts.

Summing Up

Let's review what we've covered so far. To find those common denominators that make up your best-customer profile, identify who bought what, exactly how you got those customers, and why they bought what they did from you. The answers to these three questions will help you target your best potential customers and increase your likelihood of success. It will also help you start thinking about segments of the market that you may have overlooked before. Worksheets 2.1, 2.2, and 2.3 will help you identify the common features of your best customers and determine where to find prospects who fit that profile.

So far in the targeting step of sales, you've learned how to determine your competitive advantage and how to articulate it succinctly. You've also learned how to identify your best current customers and create a profile for the kinds of prospects you want to go after. In the next chapter you will find out how to use personal marketing techniques to generate a regular supply of qualified leads.

WORKSHEET 2.1

Common Characteristics of My Best Customers

Fill in the blanks for your top customers, then look for patterns such as which industry or market segment dominates the list, who is often the ultimate decision maker, and so on.

What My Best Customers Have in Common	
Business-to-Business	**Direct-to-Consumer**
Geography	Age
Type of business	Income
Average purchase amount	Occupation
Principal contact	Zip code
Industry/SIC code	Form of payment

WORKSHEET 2.1 (continued)

What My Best Customers Have in Common	
Business-to-Business	**Direct-to-Consumer**
Size (number of employees, offices, sales volume)	Family size
Ultimate decision maker	Decision maker
Products bought from us (amount, dollar value)	Products purchased
How we got their business	Rent/own
Other	Other

WORKSHEET 2.2

Common Denominator Summary

Based on the information you outlined in Worksheet 2.1, list the characteristics of your best customers *in rank order.*

The Profile of My Best Customers Looks Like This:

	Characteristics
1.	
2.	
3.	
4.	
5.	
6.	
7.	
8.	
9.	
10.	
11.	
12.	
13.	
14.	
15.	

WORKSHEET 2.3

Finding New Best Customers

Given what you now know about the profile of your best customers, list below all the possible sources where you can find large numbers of prospects who have the same profile as your best customers.

CHAPTER 3

Using Personal Marketing to Generate Leads

Now that you can state your competitive advantage and know where to find high-quality prospects, you need to know how to generate leads. We use a simple but very effective two-step approach: First, we'll show you ways to gain visibility with your best potential customers through personal marketing so that they will contact you. Second, we'll look at ways that you can make effective contact with prospective customers. We call one method *outgoing* and the other *incoming*.

Let's define both methods before discussing them. Making a cold call on a prospective customer is outgoing, because you initiate contact with the customer. If you run an ad and the customer calls you in response, that is incoming, because the customer initiates the personal contact. And, of course, there are some grey areas between the two. If you send a direct mail letter and follow up by phone, that's outgoing. If the customer calls you before you get a chance to call her, that's incoming.

Making the distinction between outgoing and incoming is useful for several reasons. You have a much higher degree of *control* over your outgoing efforts. You can run ads in a hundred publications, but if no one calls, you have no prospects. On the other hand, the *quality* of incoming leads is usually much higher. Since they call you, they are selecting themselves as prospects for you, which usually means that they have an identified need and want your help in determining if your product or service will fill it. Let's talk first about how to get prospects to contact you.

How to Generate Incoming Leads

At one time or another in our careers we've all known an experienced, successful sales rep who seems to just sit back and respond to calls. The orders roll in, and she seems to be getting rich without effort. What we generally don't see are the many years she spent paying her dues, building her sales network, and investing in her personal visibility. She became synonymous with the product in the customers' minds. When they think of the product, they think of her. She developed a reputation as an expert ... and now she can benefit from those years of effort.

This successful salesperson is using *personal marketing*. She's marketing herself just as a company would market a product. Just as it takes time to build brand loyalty, it takes time and hard work for personal marketing to pay off, but it's worth it in the long run. How *you* will use these ideas depends to a large extent on where you are in your career. If you're just getting started you'll probably spend only 5 to 10 percent of your time on these methods because you'll need to focus more on outgoing prospecting activities covered later in this chapter. As your career and income grow, you'll want to invest more in these incoming methods until the majority of your customers are contacting you rather than the other way around. If your best potential customers have been made aware of you in advance of your contact with them through your personal marketing efforts, you'll find it much easier to set up an appointment, establish a relationship with them, and consummate the sale.

The reason it's so important to invest at least some of your time in these methods right now is that the *quality* of an incoming lead is almost always better than the quality of the lead you get on a cold call. The prospect has *already identified himself* as a probable candidate for your product. He's calling you because he has an identified need, and he wants your help in determining whether your product or service will fill it.

To gain high visibility and establish an aura of expertise, you can use a number of strategies, as shown in Figure 3.1.

Let's discuss each of these visibility strategies so that you can use them more effectively in your selling efforts. We'll skip over *personal selling* because that's what this entire book is about. We'll also skip over *direct mail* because we devote all of Chapter 4 to it. So let's now discuss each of the ten remaining visibility strategies.

Personal Advertising

First, let's talk about advertising and promoting yourself. You regularly see ads for products but rarely see ads promoting salespeople and their services, except in the real estate industry. It's common there because the salespeople are independent agents. They know that to get your listing, they have to be in your mind at the exact moment you are ready to sell your house.

If you want to have the competitive advantage in your industry or in your market area, you've got to think like an independent contractor. Depending on your target market and your company policy, you may want to run newspaper or magazine ads, or put your picture in the yellow pages.

Consider running a series of ads in a trade journal that's read by those people in your target market. You'll find that it can be very effective in building your image and making you a familiar face. Ask your customers in each industry category what trade publications they *must read* to keep up in their field. Almost every industry has at least one, and some industries have many.

Advertising Specialties

An idea that can be very powerful or a complete waste of money is *advertising specialties.* You're surely familiar with the keychains and pens that

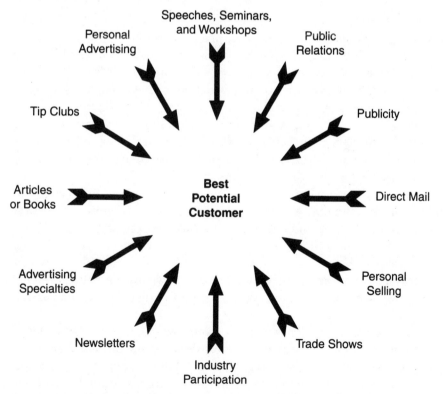

Figure 3.1 **Strategies to increase your visibility with your best potential customers**

companies give out with their names printed on them. Literally thousands of ad specialty items are available, but the key to using them is to find a gift your client will actually use or keep on his desk on a day-to-day basis that will be a powerful reminder of you and what you do.

One of the best examples of the success of this method is provided by George Walther, author of the book *Phone Power*. In his seminars, George gives away bright red, 25-foot-long coiled telephone cords, explaining that you should get up and move around while you're talking on the phone, to sound lively. People love them. They run back to the office and put their red phone cord on their anything-but-red phone, and it really stands out. Whenever someone comes into the office, they ask, "Why do you have a red cord on your phone?" A discussion of the seminar and George Walther ensues, and suddenly George has a new seminar participant, who gets a red cord, and . . . well, you get the point.

Trade Shows

Attending *trade shows* provides many practical options to generate incoming business. The best way to identify the trade shows you should attend is to ask your best customers which ones they attend. But there is a trick here. Be sure to ask your customers which ones they attend as buyers or industry members as well as those in which they are exhibitors. Each of these offers you different opportunities. At trade shows where your best potential customers attend as buyers or regular industry attendees, you can set up a booth that attracts them to stop and examine your product or service offerings.

At trade shows where your best potential customers attend as exhibitors, you can attend as a visitor and walk the floor, stopping at relevant exhibit booths to learn more about your customers' products and services. You'll also learn something about your customers' customers. You may even get to speak with some prospects whom you haven't been able to contact yet. You may even make some sales. Trade shows provide a great opportunity to see and speak with many of your best potential customers in one location in a short time.

Are we suggesting that you put up your own money to attend a trade show? Probably not, although if it's a local show you might want to consider it. We're suggesting that it's your responsibility to monitor all the trade show activity for your particular territory and target market and to work out a plan with your sales manager as to the best ways to leverage your opportunities at each show. At the very least, attend as a visitor and do some information gathering with the exhibitors. See if it would be profitable for you or your company to exhibit at this show next year. We attended the American Society for Training and Development trade show before we decided to exhibit at it. We talked to various exhibitors, including some of our competitors, to determine whether that trade show was a worthwhile investment of our limited marketing budget. Nearly everyone said it was a good investment, so we attended the following year as exhibitors and made many sales as a result of our participation.

You could even participate in a joint promotion with a noncompetitor, though you should first discuss it with your sales manager. Let's say you sell business forms. Wouldn't it make sense to begin building a partnership with companies that sell computer printers? Why not start the relationship with a joint promotion—you promote their products to your existing clients, and they promote your products to theirs? To look for possible selling partners, just think about all the related but noncompetitive products or services that your customers use in conjunction with yours.

Industry Participation

Join an association in your best target market industry. This will help you find out about trends and issues important to your best customers. Also, contact other related trade associations for their membership lists. Participate on committees to "rub elbows" with influential leaders in your key target industries.

Public Relations

Many people believe that *public relations* is supposed to be done by their company's ad agency or PR firm. For your company's products, that's probably true. But remember, we're talking about executing your *personal* public relations campaign—getting your face and name known in the community. Any community involvement counts. Consider joining a club or association or doing volunteer work. By participating in the United Way's loaned executive program, for example, you can meet and work with some of the top executives in your area. It's a real opportunity to build your network. You'll find that almost all of the local nonprofit organizations are run by the movers and shakers in your community, but don't volunteer just for the business contacts. Do it for the personal growth it'll provide and the connection with your community that you will feel. The business contacts will take care of themselves.

Keep in mind that you want to join a local or national organization in which you are likely to find people who fit the profile of your best customers. If your objective is to gain an identity in your target market nationally, a local group may not help much. Don't confuse activity with results. Salespeople who want to reach the affluent market for estate-planning products or luxury goods and services might consider joining a fund-raising group for a local symphony, opera, or theater. Many wealthy people actively participate in these groups or are the fund-raising targets for these groups.

Publicity

Publicity is aimed at generating favorable news coverage for you, your company, or your products. You do not pay for publicity, at least not directly. You can write press releases about yourself (perhaps announcing your recent promotion) or about your company (introducing a new product, for example) and send it to the business section editor of the local newspaper. You might even write a column for a target trade journal, magazine, newsletter, or newspaper, or even submit letters to the editor, to generate positive visibility.

Speeches, Seminars, and Workshops

Another way to get involved in civic and professional organizations is as a *guest speaker*. This is a great way to reach a large number of prospective customers in a short time. But remember, as a speaker your goal is to educate, not to sell. You want to make your listeners enlightened buyers, and you want them to recognize and remember you as the expert in this field so that when they are ready to buy, they come to you.

Another good way to raise your visibility and establish yourself as an expert is to conduct free (or almost free) *seminars or workshops*. This method has worked very well in the brokerage industry. Investors and potential investors are invited to a free seminar on how to structure a portfolio or how to do technical stock analysis or to hear a famous investment guru speak. Attorneys and accountants have also found do-it-yourself seminars to be very profitable, because once the attendees see the complexity of the issue involved they'll often ask the expert to handle it for them. One of our friends is a financial advisor in San Diego. One of his best markets is doctors. He frequently speaks at their meetings on financial planning strategies. As a result, doctors are constantly calling him for help with their financial planning because his speaking engagements have given him such high visibility.

Even if seminar or workshop participants don't contact you right away, you'll still be establishing your image as an expert. A local college once scheduled us for a seminar and mailed over ten thousand flyers to local businesses. An executive from one of the businesses called and engaged us to do extensive work with them. Ironically, the original seminar was canceled.

Tip Clubs

Networking clubs, or *tip clubs,* also provide a great way to gain leads, increase your visibility, build your network, and be perceived as an expert all at the same time. The purpose of these groups is to make each member aware of the resources available from the other members. This type of give-and-take results in group synergism. Each person is able to bring to the group his or her area of expertise, centers of influence, social networks, and business contacts. With everyone bouncing ideas off one another, a kind of professional kinetic energy develops in which everyone can gain information, cross-sell, obtain referrals, and increase the drive to achieve.

A tip club's membership usually consists of professionals, business owners, executives, managers, and salespeople in numerous business categories such as advertising, banking, real estate, insurance, consulting, office products, printing, stockbrokerages, travel agencies, and so on. The best tip clubs are generally limited to one member from each field of business. They usually meet once a week for breakfast or lunch. Each member brings at least one lead that will benefit other members. It might be a general lead like letting them all know that a new hotel will be built in town, or it might be a specific referral to another salesperson. The best tip clubs are fairly large and have one salesperson from each of many categories.

To find a tip club in your area, ask other salespeople you know, check with your local chamber of commerce, or start your own. Your tip club will grow quickly if the leads are of good quality. It's a great forum for promoting your business economically, efficiently, and effectively. Your fellow members become your sales force because they are constantly looking for ways to help you expand your business, and they can also become your customers.

Newsletters

Writing and distributing *newsletters* can be an excellent personal marketing tool. The key is to make them valuable to the reader, not just a sales message disguised as a newsletter. If the newsletter is full of stuff that's interesting only to you, others won't read it. But if it's full of must-know product or industry information, it will be read and saved. Keep it short. If you make it too long, people will put it aside. Don't forget to include some cartoons and pictures for variety.

Articles or Books

Now we come to one of our favorites: *publish an article* in a trade journal that your best potential customers might read. It immediately establishes you as an expert because an outside source (the trade journal) has recognized you as an expert. Besides giving you the initial exposure, it can become part of your personal brochure when you meet new clients, or you can use it as a direct mail piece. Many publications pay an honorarium for each article they publish. We often exchange the honorarium for an ad in the same issue in which our article appears. It's a one-two punch that really increases visibility and sales.

After you've written several articles, you can turn them into a book. If you can't interest a publisher, self-publish it. It'll really enhance your credibility as an expert in your field. Publishing a book may sound like an unattainable goal for most salespeople, but it's not as difficult as most people think. Talk to someone who's already been published to get some guidance. Tony just wrote a book with Garry Schaeffer entitled *Publish and Flourish: How to Boost Visibility and Earnings Through a Publishing Strategy*. If you want to take advantage of a publishing strategy in your own field, get a copy of Tony's book and make it a reality.

You may wonder what you could write about. To get a better idea of a potential topic for your book, answer these questions: What do you know well? In what areas are you an expert? What questions do your customers and prospects ask regularly? If they are confused, maybe others in their situation are too.

Develop a Prospecting Plan

Whatever sources you use, the key to good lead generation is planning. Remember, generating leads is a long-term activity that must be continuous

WORKSHEET 3.1
Visibility Strategies

Write down several techniques you intend to use to increase your exposure and generate more prospects.

1. Visibility strategy: _____

    A. _____

    B. _____

    C. _____

2. Visibility strategy: _____

    A. _____

    B. _____

    C. _____

3. Visibility strategy: _____

    A. _____

    B. _____

    C. _____

4. Visibility strategy: _____

    A. _____

    B. _____

    C. _____

5. Visibility strategy: _____

    A. _____

    B. _____

    C. _____

if you are to be a successful salesperson. Use the visibility strategies (Worksheet 3.1) to determine which techniques you'll use in your day-to-day selling efforts.

To make sure that your visibility strategies all work together, you'll need a *plan*. You need to look at what you'll do to gain visibility with each of your target market segments. And put your plan in *writing*. Evaluate the plan from time to time and update it. You'll get great results with some activities, less with others. So periodically examine and reevaluate the plan . . . build on what works and modify what doesn't. Remember, the whole point is to get your customers calling *you!*

Keep in mind that it's better to work on getting *multiple exposures to a smaller target group* than to spread your efforts and have *fewer exposures to more people*. Potential customers in your target markets should be reading your articles, receiving direct mail from you, hearing you speak or give a seminar, bumping into you at a social function or trade show, and hearing about you and your expertise from their fellow association members and friends in the form of referrals and testimonials.

Targeting a market means that you *focus* your limited marketing budget on those market segments most likely to buy from you so you'll get more "bang for the buck." When you effectively use these personal marketing ideas, you'll find that little by little, people will start to recognize your name, your company, your product, and your face. Pretty soon your phone will start ringing, and your image as an established expert will take hold. That's the power of personal marketing . . . and it's one more competitive advantage for you!

Outgoing Prospecting for Customer Leads

As you gain personal visibility and establish long-term customer relationships, incoming leads and customer referrals will come your way, but you can't sit back and wait for them. Part of your daily routine must include *outgoing* prospecting. You can find numerous ways to uncover new markets and establish new business contacts. There is no "best" strategy. They all work, so find the ones that work best for you, your product, your company, and your industry.

There are innumerable *directories* to the businesses in your industry and geographical location. Your local library and chamber of commerce are invaluable resources. If you are not familiar with their directories and indexes, ask for help.

Prospects are everywhere. Be observant. Keep your eyes, ears, and mind open to the people and situations around you. You never know when your expertise will be needed. The following paragraphs provide a few ideas on how to conduct outgoing prospecting.

Contact your satisfied customers   One of the many sources of prospects includes *satisfied customers*. These are people with whom you have business relationships. You should systematically contact them to see if they have additional needs. Satisfied customers are such an easy market to reach that they frequently slip through the cracks. Keep in mind different departments and divisions, parent companies, and other spin-offs of your present customers. In addition, when your company introduces new products or services, your entire customer list becomes a prospect list. At least once a year you should go through your customer list and a list of your products and services to see if new opportunities exist.

Investigate company leads   *Company leads* are another excellent source. Often your company will provide leads from ads, direct mail responses, telephone campaigns, and other valuable sources. These leads are generally of high quality because the prospect has already expressed an interest in your company. In this case, don't procrastinate; get back to the prospect quickly.

Talk to influential members of your community   *"Centers of influence"* are prominent people in your community who can direct you toward new prospects. A center of influence may be a priest, rabbi, minister, congressperson, attorney, banker, or prominent businessperson. Focus on building a trusting relationship with these people before asking for referrals. Be sure they know the benefits you have provided other customers. Let them know your goals so they can be aware of the kind of prospects you're looking for.

Give them a formal presentation describing your product or service. Provide them with an extensive list of testimonials, personal and business references, and a professional résumé. Centers of influence are interested in referring only those salespeople who will not undermine their reputations. Be sure to report back to the center of influence after you contact the person they referred to you. And finally, find a professional way to reciprocate or to say thank you.

Recontact former customers   *Orphan accounts* are former customers who for some reason have stopped buying. Often it's because the salesperson who was handling their account has left the company, or they may have stopped doing business with the company because of a product or service problem. If you can solve the problem, you have a good chance of winning back the account for yourself. These accounts represent a gold mine right under your nose.

Monitor and Measure Your Prospecting Efforts

Whether you are using incoming or outgoing prospecting techniques, create a system for monitoring and measuring your efforts. The more organized you are, the less likely you are to lose names and numbers, forget about prospecting, or make other costly mistakes. The first step is to set up a file for each prospect. Keep track of everything about the prospect, including dates of contact, who referred you, possible needs or opportunities, and so on.

Include in your system the steps you will take with each prospect. To organize your client and prospect files, consider this system:

- Use hanging files with 8½″ × 11″ file folders.
- Label 26 of the files A to Z. These will be your master files for your client list. You can either maintain a separate master prospect file or, if you have room, combine them with present clients.
- Give each client a separate page and record all the permanent information you have on the company—the decision maker, your contacts, addresses, phone numbers, birthdays, spouses' names, everyone's hobbies, the dog's name, and so on. Attach a contact report to this master sheet. Every time you talk to this client, make a note of the reason, the outcome, and the date of your next contact.

To remember *when* to contact customers, set up a tickler file. You probably have one already, but consider using some of our ideas to improve it. You can use a notebook, 8½ × 11 hanging file folders, or a small card file. Whatever system you use, divide it into 12 months. Also, designate a section for the current month and divide it into four or five weeks. For each client or prospect, write the client's name and contact date on an index card. As you plan contacts and follow-ups, simply put the cards in the appropriate week and mark the dates on the master sheet for each prospect or client. At the end of each week, spend some time reviewing the upcoming week's calls and put those cards in your daily reminder, notebook, or daily tickler file.

After you contact a customer, enter your notes on the contact report and put the tickler file card in the week of the next contact. There is a good reason to keep your master files and tickler files separate. Imagine you are in your office and a client calls. You quickly have to dig up your information on the account. If that information is in alphabetical order in the master file, you know exactly where to look. If it were attached to the tickler card and filed under a date somewhere in the future, you would not know where to find it unless you happened to remember when you were going to recontact that person.

Setting up a system like this may seem like a headache; however, it is worth the effort. There are also some alternatives. You could solicit the help of a well-organized friend. You could use one of the many computer programs that will organize you. You could also work with a secretary who can take the paperwork off your desk and put it in files rather than piles. Your secretary can also update your files and keep you from interfering with the system. If you choose the last idea, an efficient and time-saving tactic is to dictate the information and have it transcribed and filed.

Summing Up

No matter what system you use, it is absolutely essential to follow through with your prospects. Always keep the ball in your court. Don't expect prospects to call you back. If you spend the time to follow through, you will find your appointment book filling up with new names and numbers.

Identifying your best prospects and setting up lead-generation systems that provide you with a steady stream of prospects to talk to is the first step in the sales process. The next step is to *contact* the prospects. The next section will help you understand how to make each contact with a prospect or customer more effective.

STEP II

Contacting Your Prospect

Once you know how to identify prospective customers, you need to contact them with your message. When you come right down to it, there are really only three ways to contact a potential customer—by mail, by phone, and in person. If you want to get fancy you could include telegrams, electronic mail, and fax, but they're really just other forms of mail. Direct mail is an excellent technique for breaking the ice with a prospect and beginning to build an image of credibility and reliability. Direct mail can take the cold out of cold calling.

As the cost of in-person sales calls escalates, more and more salespeople are using the phone to reduce (and in some cases eliminate) costly face-to-face sales calls. Good phone skills combined with a well-structured direct mail program can provide you with high-quality personal appointments that naturally lead to sales.

Once you've obtained an appointment with a golden prospect who meets all your criteria, you want that appointment to flow easily and effortlessly into an exploration of the prospect's needs and concerns. This flow depends on the quality of the relationship you build, which depends on your ability to understand how your prospect wants to be treated. Spending a great deal of time talking about family and hobbies to a fast-paced, task-oriented person can destroy all your previous efforts. The chapter on relationship strategies will help you know how to adapt your actions and communications to the needs of the person you are dealing with.

The old adage, "You never get a second chance to make a good first impression," is the truth behind the contact stage. A successful sale is like building a pyramid; each step depends upon the success of the previous ones, and no step can be omitted without creating disaster.

CHAPTER 4

Contacting Prospects with Direct Mail

The first contacting method we'll look at is direct mail. When we speak of direct mail, we don't mean the huge mailings of hundreds or thousands of pieces that your company might send as part of its advertising program. These mailings generally do not involve personal or phone follow-up. The direct mail process we're talking about as part of the contacting stage of selling includes a well-thought-out letter, addressed to your best potential customers, with a phone follow-up.

Have you ever been in a sales slump? Sales are booming, then all of a sudden they fall through the floor. Most salespeople tell us that happens because they get so busy working with prospects, negotiating deals, and demonstrating the product or service that they don't have time to make contacts with new prospects. The sales pipeline empties, and there are no interested prospects left to work with! Almost all sales slumps are caused by the lack of a consistent system for prospecting.

The reason our system works so well is that it keeps you from ever having to make a cold call again. While there are some salespeople who claim they love cold calling, we've found that most salespeople view cold calling in the same way most of us view rattlesnakes and warts. Cold calling always involves a great deal of rejection, and most of us want to avoid rejection; therefore, we avoid cold calling. Success in sales requires consistent prospecting, but that does not mean cold calling! By using the direct mail program described in this chapter, you can keep your sales pipeline full of interested prospects and avoid periodic sales slumps.

One of the first things you have to understand, however, is *selective perception*. Every day we are bombarded with thousands of messages. To keep us from going crazy with information overload, our brains filter out most of the messages and let through only those that trigger recognition or need. This filtering process is called selective perception, and we all use it every day. To demonstrate how selective perception works, let's use an experience that most of us have had. Think about the last time you began shopping for a car. As soon as you decided you were in the market for a car, you suddenly started noticing automobile ads everywhere—billboards, magazines, newspapers, radio. It almost seemed as if you couldn't turn around without seeing a car ad. Then you picked out the car you wanted. Suddenly, you saw that same car . . . sometimes even the same color . . . everywhere. Everyone seemed to have one. Why hadn't you noticed before? Selective perception. Your brain was filtering these messages out until you decided you needed a car. Then your brain started to let in all those messages about cars.

Establishing a Direct Mail Campaign that Gets Your Prospect's Attention

How does the concept of selective perception apply to your use of direct mail? Well, most salespeople send one piece of direct mail and hope that:

- It gets read.
- It appeals to the reader's need.
- The reader will take action to get the product or service or will remember it by the time the salesperson gets around to calling.

Don't bet on it! In a society saturated with advertising, 15 seconds after someone hears or reads your message, he is being bombarded with the next message.

If the reader gets the first letter and it passes through his need filter . . . great! He'll call you! But what if he doesn't?

Let's take a look at what typically happens. Your prospect gets your letter, glances at it, and throws it away. Say you send a follow-up letter. The prospect gets it and says (subconsciously), "I've heard of this guy some-place before." Assume that you understand marketing and psychology enough to send a third letter. The prospect says, "You know, I've heard a lot about this company. Maybe I should give them a call."

You bet he's heard a lot about this company! And it's all been good, because he's heard it all from *you!* So what happens when you call and ask for an appointment? You're credible. You're not just another salesperson. You're a consultant with expertise in a field in which the prospect now has an interest. Studies have repeatedly shown that when a person hears about *you*, your *company*, or your *product* four or more times, they perceive you as credible. Your direct mail system sets you up as an expert so you can make warm calls on hot prospects, which beats cold calling any day of the week! The following paragraphs describe exactly how you can make this system work.

Mail three letters to each prospect   To begin, send three different letters, one week apart, to each prospect. Then call for an appointment three to five days after the last letter. This direct mail strategy might sound overwhelming as a general prospecting tool, but it can be quite successful if you use it with the top 10 percent of your prospects, the ones who can deliver up to 80 percent of your sales volume and profit. This ideal group of prospects is well worth the time, money, and effort this highly successful direct mail technique requires.

Mail to four new prospects every day   Every day, select four new prospective customers from your target market with whom you have never spoken and send them letter number one. This is the magical part of the system that ensures you'll always have a fresh supply of prospects.

Let me caution you here. Salespeople, being ever optimistic, often say, "Well, if four a day is good, a hundred a day is better!" And they soon find themselves so far behind on their calls that by the time they get around to following up, the prospect has forgotten about the letters. Another reason to send only four is that even during your busiest season, there is no excuse for not following up on your four new prospects for that day. This system takes only a few minutes a day and has tremendous payoffs . . . *but you must work the system every day.*

Those of you who are quick at math have already figured out that after the first couple of weeks you will be sending out 12 to 16 letters each day. You will be sending letter one to new prospects, letter two to last week's prospects, letter three to the prospects from two weeks ago, and so on. In a few minutes, we'll tell you how to set up a system on your personal computer or word processor so the whole process will take only a few minutes a day, but first let's talk about the direct mail piece itself.

Make your letters look personal   What does personal mail look like? It is addressed by hand or typewriter, not with a mailing label. It is preferably hand stamped. Using a postage meter immediately identifies it as business mail, but this is acceptable today because it is in such widespread use. A personal letter either has no return address or has just the address but not the company name and logo. The return address should also be typed or handwritten. For a little twist, use a simple address printed on the back flap.

Include a free gift with your letter   Making it look personal ensures that it gets opened, but how do you make sure it gets opened *first*? Make it lumpy! Why? The prospect gets her mail and says, "What could that lump possibly be? It must be a gift . . . for me!" Why would she want to open bills when she could be opening presents? She'll always open it first or last, and in either case you've got her undivided attention! How do you make your mail lumpy? Include a cassette, a video, an advertising specialty, or a sample of your product. It doesn't really matter as long as it's related to your message.

Make sure your prospect gets your message   How about the layout and copy of the actual letter? Well, you're going to use the same statement of competitive advantage that you developed earlier. Whenever you are introducing yourself to a client, regardless of whether it's in person, on the phone, or by mail, you are going to use the same basic positioning statement or a variation. Here are a few examples on pages 49, 50, 51, and 52.

Sample Letter #1

What Do Xerox, IBM, and Mercedes-Benz Have in Common?

Dear _____:

They all use the Herald Newspaper to enhance their image throughout the San Diego area . . . and increase their overall sales.

They've told us that our extensive circulation coupled with the high quality of our subscribers makes us the most effective medium in San Diego County for their advertising dollar.

If you would like to discuss some strategies for getting our readers into your store, please call me at 123–4567.

Sincerely,

Rick Barrera

P.S. Our upcoming real estate issue may be of special interest to you. It will be out the first week of December.

Sample Letter #2

Your Kids Can Be the Most Popular Kids on the Block!

Dear _____:

Have you ever noticed how kids just naturally gravitate to certain homes in your neighborhood? It seems like there's always one house that is sort of a kid magnet. Why is that?

Perhaps it's the parents, the location, a big yard, or maybe that there's always something to do at that house . . . but whatever the reason, there's a big payoff to the parents and to the kids who live there.

It's the development of social skills. A Carnegie Foundation Study showed that 85% of success in life comes from our ability to deal effectively with other people, so the earlier we learn these important skills, the better off we are.

Give your kids the edge. Make your house the neighborhood center with a Sunshine Playground.

Sincerely,

Tony Alessandra

P.S. There's an even bigger benefit to *you*. You don't ever have to wonder where your kids are!

Sample Letter #3

January 4, 1995

Julie Larson
XYZ Corporation
123 First Avenue
San Diego, CA 92121

I've Got a Real $100 Bill with Your Name on It!

Dear Ms. Larson:

I'd be willing to bet you know someone who's moving. Whether they're moving into town or out of town, I'll give you a $100 bill for everyone you refer who buys or sells a house with me.

They win because they get a Realtor who is knowledgeable and really cares . . . you win by helping them and getting your bonus . . . and I win because I made two new friends! Think about it, ask your spouse or friends who they know who's moving, and then call me with their names and numbers. I promise they'll be treated like royalty.

Sincerely,

John Lee

P.S. Call me to receive two free movie tickets I have reserved for you, good at any local theater. No obligation!

Sample Letter #4

January 4, 1995

Julie Larson
XYZ Corporation
123 First Avenue
San Diego, CA 92121

Are You Tired of Playing Telephone Tag
and Feeling Like You Are Always It?

Dear Ms. Larson:

Do you ever get tired of calling people who are not there? Or getting back to your office to find a mountain of pink messages? There is a better way!

Put a phone in your car. Yes, a cellular phone. For a lot less than you think, you can stop playing telephone tag and get rid of those pink slips forever.

But then, what would you do with all that extra time? Well, I'll bet you could think of something.

If you would like to try a phone in your car for sixty days with no rental fee, call me at 555-1234.

Sincerely,

Jim Cathcart

P.S. Ask me how you can get a free phone on our executive referral program.

I'm sure you noticed that we used a headline and included a P.S. on each letter. Research has shown that most people will read the headline and the P.S. before any other parts of the letter. They are the prime locations of your message, so always put a stand-alone benefit message in the headline and a related benefit message in the P.S. By stand-alone, we mean that if the prospect just read the headline and the P.S., he would get a complete message about your company, your product, or you. It's important that the reader be able to scan the letter and determine what the product or service is, and what the offer is. It's also important to have a call to action. Remember, your primary objective is *recognition*.

Your direct mail is limited only by your imagination. If you think your letters are fun and focused on creating opportunities or solving problems for your clients, odds are your prospects will too. If you think they are dull, so will your clients. Write several sample letters and ask three of your current customers who match your target audience to read and critique them. Use their feedback to make changes because they'll be your best predictors of the actual results you'll get with your direct mail.

Include a reply card   Always include a postage-paid reply card as well as a toll-free or local phone number to make it easier for the prospect to respond. With the new 800 long-distance services available, businesses of any size can now have 800 service *without* adding additional phones lines. Be sure to print your 800 number on the reply card as well as on the cover letter. People will often reach for the reply card to respond and then realize it's easier just to call.

Organizing Your Direct Mail System

Now we'll show you how to make the whole system work with a minimum of hassle. If you have a computer, type in each of your three different prospecting letters. If you don't have a computer, find a printer or secretarial service that does. Then enter the names and addresses of your 80 new prospects into your computer. (That's four per day multiplied by 20 working days in a month.)

Print out all 240 letters at once, but stagger the dates you print on them so that they can be sent out on the appropriate dates. (If you are using a data base computer program, the three dates can be added to the prospect's data record. If you're not, it will take a little time to stagger the dates for all 240 letters, but it makes the rest of the month extremely simple.) Stuff all the envelopes. Before you seal them, write the date that is printed on each letter on the upper-right-hand corner of the envelope where the stamp goes. Then, each day all you need to do is pull all the envelopes with today's date, put stamps on them, and drop them into the mail. To make the phone follow-up easier, print out a list of the dates that each prospect receives letter number three so you know when to call.

Summing Up

That's our simple system for creating an on-going stream of high-quality prospects. Let's review the key points:

1. Send three different letters to each prospect, one week apart.
2. Mail to four new prospects every single day.
3. Make it look personal.
4. Make it lumpy.
5. Always include a headline and a P.S.
6. Always include a reply card and a toll-free number.
7. Follow up by phone three to five days after the prospect receives your last letter.
8. Computerize your system for ease and efficiency.

Last, but most important, *work your system every day.*

Worksheets 4.1 and 4.2 will get you started with your direct mail program.

Direct mail systems don't work overnight, but they do work over time. For some businesses it can take six months or more before you see the real benefits of this effort. Be patient, and you will be handsomely rewarded. And don't forget that direct mail is not a science, it's an art. So test everything you do to see what works for you. You may not need to send three letters. You may get the same results with one or two . . . or it may take you four. You may get the same results with or without the lumps. Experiment! Have fun! The system can't possibly work if you don't use it. So get started today!

WORKSHEET 4.1
Direct Mail Preparation

Answer the following questions in preparation for writing a direct mail letter.

Target market: _____

Specifically, who within the company will you attempt to contact? Why? How will you get that person's name and title?

Person: _____

Why: _____

_____

How: _____

_____

Answer these questions that your reader will have:

1. What is the offer you're making? _____

_____

2. Exactly what will your product or service do for the reader? ____

_____

_____

3. What is the problem or opportunity? _____

_____

4. How can your products or services help with this problem or opportunity? _____

_____

5. What are your competitive advantages? _____

_____

_____

6. What action should your reader take to get the product or service? _____

_____

WORKSHEET 4.2
Direct Mail Letter

Focus for this letter: _____

_____

_____

■ Headline: _____

_____

_____

_____

■ Fun/unique points for body of letter: _____

_____

_____

_____

_____

_____

_____

_____

_____

■ P.S.: _____

_____

_____

■ Enclosure to make it lumpy: _____

_____

_____

_____

CHAPTER 5

Getting an Appointment

O nce your prospective customers have received your letters, you'll need to follow up on the phone. The telephone is potentially your most efficient and profitable marketing tool. When you are selling on the phone, you don't have time to waste. You must be a polished professional. For that reason, we're going to review the basics that most salespeople get out of the habit of doing. Vince Lombardi, the late, great coach of the Green Bay Packers, used to say to his champion teams on the first day of practice, "Gentlemen, this is a football." We'll start the same way: Salespeople, this is a telephone. Learning how to use it effectively will increase your income and give you another competitive advantage!

As a professional salesperson, you prepare before going to meet with a prospect in person. You do some research on him and his company. You plan your strategy and prepare some questions to ask. You make sure you have your competitive advantage or initial benefit statement ready, and you have familiarized yourself with some key phrases or jargon that demonstrates your understanding of the prospect's industry. You have thought through any initial resistance he might bring up and have facts, studies, or references ready to help him past those resistances. So why should phone contact be any different? Unfortunately, many salespeople treat it differently. They find a prospect's name, pick up the phone, and wing it. Then they complain that they have a hard time getting prospects interested over the phone.

How to Get Your Prospect on the Phone

Although phone calls don't have the advantage of your being able to see the prospect's environment and don't give you the chance to make as much of a personal impression, they can be a highly effective part of your sales process. Preparing for the telephone call just as you would for the in-person call will make a big difference in your results. Each time a prospect gets on the phone with you, you have an opportunity to create a new lifetime customer. Being prepared ensures that you will maximize that opportunity.

Being effective on the phone includes finding out who the best person is to speak with, getting her on the phone, and then engaging her in your idea in such a way that she'll want to learn more in a face-to-face meeting. And remember, if you miss on any of the three, you're out. That's why absolute proficiency in this area is critical. Here are some ideas on how to get through to your prospect when you phone:

Call the company and ask to speak with the president's secretary This is of one of the best ways to get someone to take your call. Ask the secretary for the name of the person who is responsible for making an executive-level decision for your type of product or service. Then call that person and use the president's secretary's name during your introduction. Another good way to get through the company screen is to call the switchboard and ask for the direct-dial number of the person you are calling. Then call back using his direct-dial extension.

Call before or after regular business hours, or at lunchtime   Many executives go in early or stay late. You'll often find the assistant isn't there to screen the call. At lunchtime, you'll find a fill-in who generally won't screen the call . . . and don't forget to try Saturday mornings when many executives go in to work.

Don't hang up on voice mail   Many salespeople make this mistake. Voice mail gives you an opportunity to speak directly to your potential customer at a time when he is ready to hear it. Pay close attention to the personality and style of the outgoing message he leaves, and match his style and pacing in your message. Give your name, company, and number first, then your message, and your name and number again so he won't have to replay your message to get the number.

Ask the person who referred you (if your lead is a referral) to call on your behalf   This call could be to set an appointment or introduce you. Perhaps you could try a conference call so the person referring you could tell the prospect why she is recommending you.

What if you get your prospect's assistant?   Ask for the prospect by first name only in a very casual manner. The assistant may perceive you as a personal friend and not bother to screen the call. But never lie. Don't say it's personal if it isn't. If that doesn't work, make the assistant your ally. Asking if the person is an assistant, rather than a secretary, will get the relationship off to a good start. Find out his or her name; show respect. Tell the assistant your situation and ask for help. State your name and company clearly. Give the reason for your call. If you initially sent a direct mail letter, you might say that you are following up on correspondence you sent recently and that the prospect is expecting your call. The prospect should be, since you stated in your direct mail letter that you would be following up by phone.

Be sure to acknowledge that you are concerned about not wasting the boss's time. You're calling to spend just a minute or so on the phone to determine if any further follow-up is needed. If now isn't a good time, when does the assistant think it might be convenient? Would it be possible to make a phone appointment at that time?

Try contacting your prospect by fax   If your prospect isn't in when you call, find out when she'll return and call back. If you're really having a hard time getting through, try the fax. Most offices don't have a procedure yet for screening faxes. But make the fax message a short statement of benefit and a request for a phone or personal appointment. Do not send multiple-page messages or brochures by fax . . . doing so ties up your prospect's fax machine and can be very irritating.

Call other people in your target compny   If it looks as if you're really not going to get through, you may want to ask the assistant for the names of others inside the company who might be open to your ideas. If you can get a foot in the door, you may be able to build alliances with them that will get you an audience with the key decision maker.

Be innovative to get your prospect's attention   If everything else has failed and this is an important enough customer, consider sending your prospect a check made out to her favorite charity with a letter stating that if she'll meet with you for a few minutes, you'll sign the check. If you really want to get creative, you can send balloons or flowers to your prospect with a note saying, "I have an idea that will send your business sky-high" or "I'm sure our relationship would bloom if we could speak for a few minutes." Use your imagination and have some fun. If you've done your homework and know that your product or service would have benefit for this prospect, these creative approaches can pay big dividends.

Remember to watch your investment of time, energy, and money, because it might make more sense to just move on to another prospect. We have a rule: Three calls and a letter or fax, then try something creative or follow up in three to six months. Things may have changed dramatically by then.

It's also important to remember that the purpose of your call is not to make a sale, it's to begin building a long-term relationship. You want an appointment so you can get to know your prospect and his needs. Use Worksheet 5.1 to help you plan your initial telephone approach to improve your chances of getting an appointment with your prospects.

Keep a Phone Log to Track Your Results

We also recommend you monitor and measure your calls. To improve any skill, you need a baseline against which you can chart your progress. To increase your effectiveness on the telephone, keep track of your calls. A daily and weekly telephone log (see Worksheets 5.2 and 5.3) will help you structure the data you should keep pertaining to each calling session. This log is not concerned with individual accounts. It is a day-by-day tally of what happened with each call you made. The importance of keeping a log is in the analysis of the results. Let's say, for example, you chose a different time to make your calls every day for two weeks. At the end of that time, your log would show you which times were productive and which were not. If you found you had to call a customer an average of three times before getting through, you may be calling at the wrong time. If you find you're getting through to your prospects but are not getting appointments, you should analyze your telephone habits. Without a telephone log, you won't be able to see the patterns and analyze your performance.

Overcoming a Prospect's Initial Resistance

Now let's discuss those up-front objections you receive, like "I'm not interested" or "I'm happy with my current supplier." Most up-front objections are avoidance tactics. The prospect doesn't want to talk to you because he's afraid you are going to pressure him. His way of avoiding the pressure is to hit you with objections that he hopes are difficult to counter.

If you have done a good job targeting your prospects, you know there is a good chance your product or service will interest your prospect. So you need to get past those up-front objections. Open with your competitive advantage statement and be sure it contains a specific benefit for this customer. Suppose you're selling a cost accounting system for hospitals. You might say, "Our case mix management module is used by over 40 percent of the hospitals your size, and last year those hospitals reported savings averaging 18 percent." To make that introduction even more powerful, give him the name of someone who referred him. A familiar name is a powerful ice-breaker . . . especially if it's the name of a respected peer.

WORKSHEET 5.1
Planning an Initial Phone Contact

Use this worksheet to plan what you will say to one of your prospective customers. It will also serve you in the future as a planning sheet for your phone calls to set appointments with prospective customers.

1. Target market segment: _____

2. Include your competitive advantage statement

   (from Worksheet 1.1):

   _____

   _____

   _____

3. Purpose (objective) for calling: _____

   _____

4. Key points to cover: _____

   _____

5. Key information to discover: _____

   _____

6. Possible customer concerns: _____

   _____

7. Answer to customer concerns: _____

   _____

8. What commitment will you ask this prospect to make? _____

   _____

WORKSHEET 5.2
Daily Call Log

Use a copy of the forms on pages 62 and 63 for 30 days to track your calling patterns.

Date	Time	Customer	Results

WORKSHEET 5.3

Weekly Call Log

Record the number of calls every day and the number of actual contacts. Use hash marks (┼┼┼┼) to record your calls and contacts. At the end of each day and week, write the totals in the space provided.

	Mon	Tues	Wed	Thurs	Fri	Weekly Total
Week 1						
Calls						
Total calls						
Contacts						
Total contacts						
Week 2						
Calls						
Total calls						
Contacts						
Total contacts						
Week 3						
Calls						
Total calls						
Contacts						
Total contacts						
Week 4						
Calls						
Total calls						
Contacts						
Total contacts						

"I Don't Need What You're Selling"

When the prospect says he has no *need*, you have to let him know you won't try to sell him anything unless you can clearly show how you can help him—help him increase profits, decrease costs, or increase productivity. Let him know that the purpose of your call is to begin building a mutually beneficial business relationship and to learn more about him and his company so you can be more specific about the benefits he'll receive.

You might also say something like this: "It's funny you should say that. I just finished installing one of our systems for Ms. Collins at Oak Bridge Hospital. Initially she didn't think she needed it either, but after we showed her the results of our free system review, she realized she did have a need after all. Could I offer you a free system review?"

"I'm Too Busy to See You Now"

If your prospect is too busy or has no time to see you now, you can ask to schedule an appointment at a more convenient time, or even ask for a phone interview. You might also promise not to take up any more time than he'll allow you. If at that point he wants you to leave, you will. But if he wants you to stay longer to complete your collaborative sales process, you'll be more than happy to do so. The decision on how long you'll stay is totally dependent on him. As a sweetener you might also offer breakfast, lunch, dinner, or a ride to the airport when he takes his next trip. Stress that you really do want to get to know him and his business a little better and that you're willing to go out of your way to do it.

"I Don't Have Any Time to See You"

What if your prospect has no time to see you at all? You might say that's exactly why he *should* take the time to see you. This statement should be used when you sell a product or service that is more convenient, can save time, or can make the prospect more efficient, such as a computer system, a portable or mobile phone, dictation equipment, certain software, or a service that would free him of something he currently has to do himself, such as financial planning or recruiting new employees.

"I'm Satisfied with My Current Supplier"

When you come across a prospect who's happy with her current supplier, you might ask, "Of all the things you like about your present supplier, what one thing do you like the least?" Here you are looking for areas where you might have a competitive uniqueness or advantage. The objective here is to have the prospect discover for herself some discontent with her existing supplier or product. That's where you can be of help. Make sure this doesn't come across as "competition bashing," but rather as an honest attempt to discover ways you can help this prospect achieve her goals better than her current supplier can.

You can also talk about the merits of dealing with multiple suppliers for the same products. Offer just to update her on your most recent products and prices so she can keep her current supplier on his toes. You might say, "Most of my clients find competition among suppliers to be good business and an easy way to manage a vendor's service and price commitments." You may want to discuss how economic or political conditions, supply shortages, mergers, acquisitions, business failures, and so on dictate not relying on a sole supplier. Worksheet 5.4 will help you construct your answers to common up-front objections.

Making a Cold Call in Person

Now let's discuss approaching the prospect via an in-person *cold call*. Cold calling can be an excellent complement to your other forms of prospecting, especially when you're selling a product that has universal interest, such as office products or supplies, or in an area where prospects are highly concentrated, such as an office building in a major city or an office park in a small suburban area. You have the benefit of reaching many prospects in a relatively short time.

Many salespeople say that they don't make cold calls. They respond only to company-supplied leads, advertising inquiries, or referrals. But these salespeople don't realize that every call they make on a new prospect is, in a sense, a "cold" call. When the salesperson contacts the prospect, that prospect is very likely preoccupied with something else. The salesperson must therefore help prospects make a mental and physical transition from what they're doing now to what the salesperson would like them to be doing and thinking. In cold call selling, the salesperson may be competing not only with another company for that prospect's business, but, more importantly, will very likely be competing for that prospect's time and attention.

Some industries still use in-person cold calling quite effectively. For instance, we purchased a security alarm system for our home. Immediately

WORKSHEET 5.4

Common Up-Front Objections

When you make initial contact with a prospect, you frequently face up-front objections. Below are some of the most common objections salespeople typically receive. Following each objection, write what you feel is the best response to deal with that objection.

1. Objection: *"I don't need what you're selling."*

   Your response: _____

   _____

   _____

   _____

2. Objection: *"I'm too busy to see you now."*

   Your response: _____

   _____

   _____

   _____

   _____

3. Objection: *"I don't have any time to see you."*

   Your response: _____

   _____

   _____

   _____

   _____

4. Objection: *"I'm satisfied with my current supplier."*

   Your response: _____

   _____

   _____

   _____

after it was installed, the salesperson called on our neighbors to explain what kind of alarm signals they might hear. While he was offering information, he was also explaining his service and doing some very smart cold call selling. Cold calling is very effective when you have a product that appeals to universal needs, such as security alarm systems, office products, and printing.

Even in industries where in-person cold calling is not the norm, salespeople often make drop-in calls when they're in a certain vicinity and have time between appointments. A good example was our neighborhood real estate agent, who represented a national real estate company. When we bought our first home in San Diego, she stopped by to welcome us to the area. She introduced herself as our neighborhood realtor, explained her vast knowledge of the local market, and told us about her network of contacts that made it easy for her to list and sell homes specifically in our neighborhood. Every month, without fail, she'd stop by our house to say hello and drop off a newsletter on trends in the local real estate market. Without fail, she'd ask if we knew of anyone who might be interested in selling or buying a home. It took nearly 13 months, but when we were ready to sell our home and move up to a bigger one, we could think of no one better than this woman to sell our current home and take us around to help us purchase our new home. Her persistent, friendly cold calls produced two sales.

Research Your Prospect Before Making a Cold Call

One of the reasons more salespeople don't make cold calls is because of fear—typically a fear of rejection or of making fools of themselves. One of the best ways you can avoid making a fool of yourself is to be well prepared before making any cold calls. Knowing how to open the call to create prospect interest immediately is a good first step. Most of the techniques we discussed earlier are as true for in-person cold calling as for phoning. You need to make sure your first 30 seconds includes a targeted positioning statement, and whenever possible, tell the prospect who referred you. Never say, "I was just in the neighborhood." It sounds as if you had nothing better to do. Open with your positioning statement and then say, "I had planned to call you next week, but I was working with Mr. Miller at CXX right next door and we finished a little early, so I thought I'd drop by to see if we might be able to set up an appointment."

Collaborative salespeople do their homework before making cold calls. The more precall preparation the salesperson does, the less fearful and threatening the sales call becomes. It's like turning a cold call into a "warm" call. Collaborative salespeople plan and research their territories, their competitors, and their best potential customer market segments before contacting a prospect for the first time. There are many benefits to precall preparation:

- It saves time. Prospects appreciate it when you take up as little of their time as possible.
- It makes you look professional. Being organized allows you to be informed and communicate quickly and effectively.
- It reduces tension. Salespeople who are well prepared worry less about things going wrong.
- It increases your sales. The better prepared you are, the more effective you'll be in every cold call you make, and the more sales you'll be able to produce.

The preparation you do before cold calling should *focus on which geographic area* or *type of business* would be most receptive to cold calls. Once you determine the area and type of business to cold call, you'll then need to identify the specific prospects to call on—those who need your product and are able to buy. Before the initial cold call contact, you should uncover the name of the decision maker you'll have to deal with at each specific company you'll be cold calling. You can obtain this information by calling a receptionist and asking, "Who is the person responsible for . . ." or "Who is in charge of . . ." You can also ask noncompetitive salespeople who are familiar with the company the names of the key decision makers in that company. Other sources can be industry journals, annual reports, and local business newspapers.

There are several steps that you should undertake before you have cold call meetings with prospects. These steps focus your attention and creative energy and increase your success significantly:

1. Do all the research and preparation possible.
2. Write out the questions you intend to ask as well as the general topics you plan to cover during the cold call.
3. Anticipate the prospect's answers and brainstorm possible problems and opportunities that may arise.
4. Visualize your success. Spend time sitting quietly with your eyes closed, and imagine yourself with the prospect successfully achieving your objectives. This is a powerful tool that really works!
5. Role play in-person cold calls with fellow salespeople. Many salespeople avoid this exercise, but those who use it swear by it. Role

playing will sharpen your ability to anticipate questions and issues. Your role-playing partner should stretch your imagination without harassing you just for the fun of it. It's also helpful to record your role-playing session on audio- or videotape. The insight you'll gain from listening to or watching the session will be invaluable.

6. Go over your cold call objectives, ideas, questions, and overall plan of action with your sales manager. Get feedback and input as to how to improve your approach.

7. Sleep on it. You'll be amazed at what you'll think of when you let all the information percolate in your mind. You'll think of additional questions, issues, and creative ideas.

This seven-step program of precall planning will serve you well if you use it routinely. Of course, for brief cold call meetings with prospects, you need do only some of the steps.

Here's a reminder of something I'm sure you already know. It's essential to have everything ready and at your disposal when meeting with a prospect. *Plan ahead.* Take enough business cards, literature, brochures, and other documents you may need. If you'll be riding in your car with the prospect, make sure it's clean. If you'll be giving a presentation, make sure your equipment is in top working order. Photocopied documents should be stapled and carried in something that will protect them. Giving forethought to your presentation will help you avoid embarrassing surprises.

Simply stated, preparation takes the fear and the unknown out of in-person cold calls and makes them a much more effective part of your entire selling process. Generally speaking, don't expect to make a sale on your very first cold call unless you're selling a relatively inexpensive, widely used product, such as magazines, cleaning products, office supplies, and the like. What you should expect to accomplish on your first cold call is to begin establishing a relationship with the key decision maker and his or her assistant. You may also be lucky enough to gather some information about the prospect's needs and expectations that you can use to develop options and solutions for your next call.

Summing Up

You might be wondering which of the three contacting methods yields the best results—direct mail, telephone, or in-person cold calls. Most top salespeople use all three methods to reach the largest number of qualified prospects possible. Each sales situation requires its own mix of direct mail, telephone, and in-person contacts. Use your judgment and your own past experience as a guideline.

The next chapter will help you understand how to tailor each of these contact methods to the particular preferences of your prospects. It will give you a simple guide to building strong relationships with your customers.

CHAPTER 6

Strategies to Improve Your Relationships with Prospects and Customers

We've given you numerous good ideas for contacting prospects through the mail, on the phone, and in person. Now it's time to start building the face-to-face relationship with the prospect. As we said earlier: You never get a second chance to make a good first impression. So how do you make sure when you begin the actual sales call that your first contact gets the relationship started right? Should you talk about the big football game or get right down to business? Unfortunately, many salespeople choose the option they're most comfortable with while unintentionally ignoring the needs of the customer. If you treat others as you want to be treated, you may end up ignoring their needs, wants, and expectations, which may be completely different from yours.

But how do you know the way your prospects and customers want to be treated? To help simplify this critical task for you, we've developed a sales tool we call the Behavioral Style Grid. It will help you understand how best to deal with all the people in your life, especially your clients and prospects.

Determining the Behavioral Style of Your Prospects and Customers

The Behavioral Style Grid is constructed by an understanding of two dimensions of behavior: indirect versus direct, and open versus self-contained.

The first dimension is indirect/direct (see Figure 6.1). People on the *direct* side of the scale, the right-hand side, are fast-paced people who make decisions quickly, like to take risks, and are often impatient. Direct people

Directness is the way one deals with information and situations.
Summary of direct and indirect behaviors.
• They approach risk, decision, or change slowly and cautiously.
• They infrequently contribute to group conversations.
• They infrequently use gestures and voice intonation to emphasize points.
• They often make qualified statements: "According to my sources . . ." "I think so."
• They emphasize points through explanations of the content of the message.
• Their questions tend to be for clarification, support, or information.
• They reserve expression of opinions.
• They are more patient and cooperative.
• They are diplomatic.
• When not in agreement (if it's no big deal), they are most likely to go along.
• They are understated and reserved.
• Maintain intermittent initial eye contact.
• At social gatherings, they are more likely to wait for others to introduce themselves.
• They have a gentle handshake.
• They tend to follow established rules and policies.

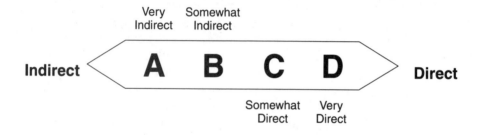

• They approach risk, decisions, or change quickly and spontaneously.
• They frequently contribute to group conversations.
• They frequently use gestures and voice intonation to emphasize points.
• They often make emphatic statements: "This is so!" "I'm positive!"
• They emphasize points through confident vocal intonation and assertive body language.
• Their questions tend to be rhetorical, to emphasize points or to challenge information.
• They express opinions readily.
• They are less patient and are competitive.
• They are confronting.
• They are more likely to maintain their position when not in agreement (argue).
• They are intense and assertive.
• They sustain initial eye contact.
• They are more likely to introduce self to others at social gatherings.
• They have a firm handshake.
• They tend to bend or break established rules and policies.

Figure 6.1 **Summary of direct and indirect behaviors.**

come on strong, take the initiative, and tend to be assertive. They tend to talk a lot and appear confident and emphatic.

Indirect people, on the left-hand side, operate at a slower, more deliberate pace. They are patient, make decisions more carefully, and avoid risk. Indirect people are more reserved and quiet, and sometimes appear indecisive when actually they merely are avoiding the risk that might result from a poor decision. They are less confronting, less demanding, and less assertive than the direct person. They are good team players and often let others take the initiative.

The other dimension is open/self-contained (see Figure 6.2). Open people, on the top side of our behavioral grid, are expressive with their thoughts and feelings. They use a lot of body language and facial expressions, and their conversations generally include a lot of stories and anecdotes. They are generally casual about time and are more interested in relationships than tasks. Their feelings play an important part in the decisions they make.

If open people are an open book, self-contained people are "poker faced." Self-contained people, on the bottom of the grid, like to keep their thoughts and emotions much more private. They keep their distance mentally and physically. Self-contained people place a high priority on getting things done and meeting deadlines. They like organization and structure and tend to make decisions based on facts.

By now you may be getting a pretty good idea of where you fall on these two scales, and you may be asking yourself which is better—direct or indirect; open or self-contained. There are no good or bad styles, there are just differences. The real question isn't which behavioral style is better, but how to best use the positive aspects of each trait while remembering that, taken to the extreme, each trait can be a drawback. We all face a variety of situations requiring different responses. What we want to do is learn when to use each behavior style.

If we put the two dimensions together, indirect to direct across, and open to self-contained top to bottom, we get a four-quadrant graph—what we call the Behavioral Style Grid and the four basic behavioral styles, illustrated in Figure 6.3. Though most people display some traits of the other styles from time to time, a person's style describes how he or she behaves most of the time.

Summary of open and self-contained behaviors.
Openness shows in the degree of self-disclosure—a person's readiness and willingness to outwardly show thoughts and feelings and accept openness from others.

Open

1 Very Open

2 Somewhat Open

3 Somewhat Self-contained

4 Very Self-contained

Self-contained

Here is a list of typical characteristics of people with open behaviors:
• They are self-disclosing.
• They show and share feelings freely.
• They make most decisions based on feelings (subjective).
• In conversations, they digress and stray from the subject.
• They are more relaxed and warm.
• They go with the flow.
• They readily express opinions and feelings.
• They are easy to get to know in business or unfamiliar social situations.
• They are flexible about how their time is used by others.
• They prefer to work with others.
• They initiate or accept physical contact.
• They share or enjoy listening to personal feelings, especially positive ones.
• Their facial expressions during speaking and listening are animated.
• They show more enthusiasm than the average person.
• They have a friendly handshake.
• They are more likely to give nonverbal feedback.
• They are responsive to dreams, visions, and concepts.

Here is a list of typical characteristics of people with self-contained behaviors:
• They are guarded.
• They keep feelings private; they share only on a "need-to-know" basis.
• They make most decisions based on evidence (objective).
• They focus conversations on issues and tasks; they stay on the subject.
• They are more formal and proper.
• They go with the agenda.
• They are fact and task oriented.
• It takes time to get to know them in business or unfamiliar social situations.
• They are disciplined about how their time is used by others.
• They prefer to work independently.
• They avoid or minimize physical contact.
• They tell or enjoy listening to goal-related stories and anecdotes.
• They have a limited range of facial expressions during speaking and listening.
• They show less enthusiasm than the average person.
• They have a formal handshake.
• They are less likely to give nonverbal feedback, if they give it at all.
• They are responsive to realities, actual experiences, and facts.

Figure 6.2 **Summary of open and self-contained behaviors.**

Four core, behavioral styles.

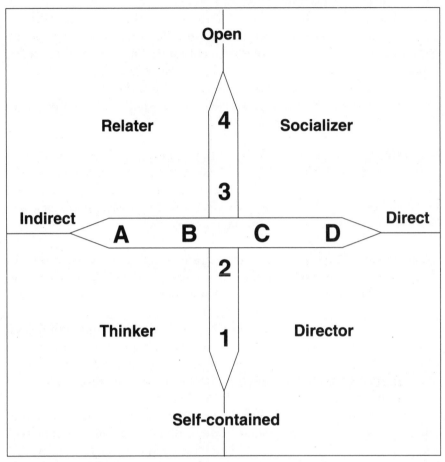

Figure 6.3 **Four core behavioral styles.**

Customers Who Are Direct and Self-Contained: Directors

In the four-quadrant graph, the lower right quadrant is where direct and self-contained overlap. We call the people who share those traits *directors*. Directors are driven by an inner need to lead and control. They want to take charge of people and situations so they can reach their goals. Their key need is achieving, so they seek no-nonsense, bottom-line results. Their motto is "Lead, follow, or get out of the way."

Directors want to win, so they often challenge people or rules. They accept challenges, take authority, and plunge headfirst into solving problems. They tend to exhibit great administrative and operational skills and work quickly and impressively by themselves. They tend to be independent, strong-willed, precise, goal-oriented, cool, and competitive with others, especially in a business environment. They try to shape their environment to overcome obstacles en route to their accomplishments. They demand maximum freedom to manage themselves and others and use their leadership skills to become winners.

Strengths   Their primary skills are their ability to get things done, lead others, and make decisions. Directors are able to focus on one task to the exclusion of everything else. They accept challenges, take authority, and expect others to do the same. They prefer to work with people who are decisive, efficient, receptive, and intelligent.

Weaknesses   Closely allied to their positive traits are the negative ones of stubbornness, impatience, and toughness. Directors have a low tolerance for the feelings, attitudes, and inadequacies of co-workers and subordinates.

Directors like to move at a fast pace and are impatient with delays. They tend to view others who move at a slower speed as incompetent. They tend to be inflexible, poor listeners, and insensitive to the needs of others. Their complete focus on their own goals and the task at hand can make them appear aloof.

The competitive nature of directors is probably typified by the statement (used by both Vince Lombardi and Red Sanders) that "Winning isn't everything . . . it's the only thing!" Directors can be so single-minded that they forget to take the time to "stop and smell the roses." And if they do remember, they may return and comment, "I smelled twelve roses today . . . how many did you smell?"

Customers Who Are Indirect and Self-Contained: Thinkers

On our grid, the bottom left quadrant is where indirect and self-contained overlap in the *thinkers*. Thinkers are detail-oriented, analytical, persistent, and systematic problem solvers. They are more concerned with content than style. Thinkers prefer involvement with products and services under specific, and preferably controlled, conditions so the performance, process, and results can be perfected.

The primary concern of cautious thinkers is accuracy. This often means that emotions take a back seat since they are subjective and tend to distort objectivity. Their biggest fear is of uncontrolled emotions and irrational acts that might prevent the achievement of their goals. Thinkers strive to avoid embarrassment by attempting to control both themselves and their emotions. They are very security conscious and have a high need to be correct, leading them to an overreliance on the collection of data.

Thinkers prefer tasks over people and like to have clearly defined priorities. They like to operate at a steady pace that allows them to check and recheck their work. They tend to see the serious, more complicated sides of situations.

Thinkers demand a lot from themselves and others and may become overly critical of themselves and others. Generally, they tend to keep their criticisms to themselves, hesitating to tell people what they think is deficient.

When thinkers have definite knowledge of facts and details, they quietly hold their ground. After determining the specific risks, margins of error, and other variables that significantly influence the desired results, they will take action.

Strengths   Strengths of cautious thinkers include accuracy, dependability, independence, clarification and testing skills, follow-through, and organization. They often focus on expectations such as policies, practices, procedures, and, of course, outcomes.

Thinkers tend to be serious and orderly and are likely to be perfectionists. They tend to focus on the details and the process of work and become irritated by surprises and glitches. They tend to be skeptical and like to see things in writing.

Weaknesses   Because thinkers need to be right, they prefer checking processes themselves. This tendency toward perfectionism taken to the extreme can result in "paralysis by overanalysis."

Thinkers can be seen as aloof, picky, and critical. Their fear of being wrong can make them overreliant on the collection of data and slow to reach a decision. Although thinkers are good listeners and ask a lot of questions, they often focus too much on details and miss the big picture.

Customers Who Are Direct and Open: Socializers

In the upper right corner of our grid, direct and open traits overlap to form the *socializers*. They're friendly, enthusiastic, and like to be where the action is. They thrive on admiration, acknowledgment, compliments, and applause. They want to have fun and enjoy life. Energetic and fast-paced socializers tend to place more priority on relationships than on tasks.

Often they're not as concerned about winning or losing as they are about how they look while they play the game. Socializers' greatest fear is public humiliation; they don't want to appear uninvolved, unattractive, unsuccessful, or unacceptable to others.

Strengths   Socializers' primary strengths are enthusiasm, persuasiveness, and friendliness. They are idea people who have the ability to get others caught up in their dreams. With great persuasion, they influence others and shape their environments by building alliances to accomplish their results.

Socializers are generally very open with their ideas and feelings. They are sometimes seen as "wearing their hearts on their sleeves." They are animated, interactive storytellers who have no qualms about "creative exaggeration." They love an audience and thrive on involvement with people. They tend to work quickly and enthusiastically with others.

Weaknesses   Their weaknesses are impatience, too much involvement, aversion to being alone, and short attention spans. This causes them to become easily bored. When a little data comes in, interacting socializers tend to make sweeping generalizations. They may not check everything out, assuming that someone else will do it, or may procrastinate because redoing something just isn't exciting enough.

When taken to the extreme, socializer behaviors can be seen as superficial, haphazard, erratic, and overly emotional. The socializer's need for acknowledgment can lead to self-absorption. They have a casual approach to time and often drive the other styles crazy with their lateness and missed deadlines. The fun-loving, life-of-the-party socializer can be undisciplined, forgetful, too talkative, and too eager for credit and recognition.

Customers Who Are Indirect and Open: Relaters

In the upper left corner of the Behavioral Grid, indirect and open traits overlap to form the *relaters*. Relaters are warm, supportive, and reliable. They are the most people-oriented of all the four styles. Having close, friendly, personal, first-name relationships with others is one of their most important objectives. They dislike interpersonal conflict so much that they sometimes say what they think other people want to hear. They have tremendous counseling skills and are extremely supportive. Relaters are excellent listeners and generally develop relationships with people who are also good listeners. As a result, they have strong networks of people who are willing to be mutually supportive.

Relaters focus on getting acquainted and building trust. Pushy, aggressive behavior irritates them. They are cooperative, steady workers, and excellent team players. They strive for security and try to maintain stability and a peaceful environment. While the unknown may be an intriguing concept, they prefer to stick with what they already know and have experienced. Risk is an ugly word to relaters. They may even stay in an unpleasant environment rather than risk a change. Disruption in their routine patterns can distress them. If they are faced with a change, they need to think it through carefully and plan for the changes. Finding elements of sameness within those changes can help minimize their stress.

Strengths   The primary strengths of relaters are relating to, caring for, and loving others. They are courteous, friendly, and willing to share responsibilities. They are good planners, are persistent, and generally follow through with their plans.

Weaknesses   Relaters have difficulty speaking up and expressing their true feelings, especially if it might create conflict. They appear to go along with others even when they inwardly do not agree. They can be overly sensitive and easily bullied.

Their need for security makes them very slow at making decisions, and this is often perceived as weakness or indecisiveness. In fact, their slowness results from their need to avoid risk and unknown situations and their desire to include others in the decision-making process.

Classifying Your Prospects and Customers

Each of your customers will fall roughly into one of these four styles on the Behavioral Style Grid—dominant directors, cautious thinkers, interacting socializers, and steady relaters. To decide which style best describes your customer, you need to make only two decisions: Is your prospect more direct or more indirect? More open or more self-contained? See Table 6.1 and Table 6.2 for a quick visual summary of these dimensions. By having

Table 6.1 Summary of Style Descriptors

	Directors	Thinkers	Socializers	Relaters
Strengths	Administration Leadership Juggling	Planning Organization Systematizing	Persuading Enthusiasm Motivation	Listening Teamwork Follow-through
Weaknesses	Impatient Insensitive to others Poor listener	Perfectionistic Critical Unresponsive	Inattentive to detail Short attention span Poor follow-through	Oversensitive Slow to begin action Poor at goal setting
Occupations	Top executive Military leader Newspaper editor	Engineer Accountant Librarian	Sales Public relations Performing artist	Family doctor Social worker Teacher
Irritations	Inefficiency Indecision	Disorganization Unpredictability	Routine Perfectionism	Insensitivity Impatience
Under stress	Dictatorial Critical	Withdrawn Headstrong	Sarcastic Superficial	Submissive Indecisive
Decisions are	Decisive	Deliberate	Spontaneous	Consultative
Seeks	Productivity	Accuracy	Recognition	Acceptance

	Fast/Decisive	Slow/Systematic	Fast/Spontaneous	Slow/Relaxed
Pace	Fast/Decisive	Slow/Systematic	Fast/Spontaneous	Slow/Relaxed
Priority	The task/Results	The task/Process	The relationship/Interaction	The relationship/Communication
Appearance	Businesslike Functional	Formal Conservative	Fashionable Stylish	Casual Conforming
Workplace	Busy Efficient Structured	Structured Functional Formal	Stimulating Personal Cluttered	Personal Relaxed Friendly
Gains security through	Control Leadership	Preparation Thoroughness	Playfulness Others' approval	Friendship Cooperation
Fears	Being taken advantage of	Criticism of their work	Loss of prestige	Sudden changes
Measures personal worth by	Results Track record Measurable progress	Precision Accuracy Activity	Acknowledgments Recognition Applause Compliments	Compatibility with others Depth of relationships
Internal motivator	Winning	The process	The chase	Involvement

81

Table 6.2 **Observable Characteristics
in the Four Behavioral Styles**

	Verbal (words)	**Vocal (tone of voice)**	**Visual (body language)**
Directors	Tell more than ask Talk more than listen Lots of verbal communication Make emphatic statements Blunt and to the point	More vocal variety More forceful tone Communicate readily High volume, faster speech Challenging voice intonation	Firm handshake Steady eye contact Use gestures to emphasize points Display impatience Fast moving
Thinkers	Fact and task-oriented Limited sharing of feelings More formal and proper Focused conversation	Little inflection Few pitch variations Less variety in vocal quality Steady, monotone delivery Low volume, slow speech	Few facial expressions Non-contact-oriented Few gestures
Socializers	Tell stories, anecdotes Share personal feelings Informal speech Express opinions readily Flexible time perspective Digress from conversation	Lots of inflection More pitch variation More variety in vocal quality Dramatic High volume Fast speech	Animated facial expressions Much hand/body movement Contact-oriented Spontaneous actions
Relaters	Ask more than tell Listen (more than talk) Reserve opinions Less verbal communication	Steady, warm delivery Less forceful tone Lower volume Slower speech	Intermittent eye contact Gentle handshake Exhibit patience Slower moving

to make only two decisions, you can quickly determine your customer's style. It's actually a process of elimination.

The first question is whether your customer is direct or indirect. Is she assertive and fast-paced? Does she make swift decisions, take risks, express opinions readily? Is she impatient and competitive? If so, she's more direct. However, if she's easygoing, quiet, reserved, and cooperative, if she asks and listens more than tells, avoids risks, and makes slower deliberate decisions, then she's indirect.

Okay, let's say that she is indirect. That means she is either a thinker or a relater; you've eliminated the direct styles of socializer and director. Now all you have to do is determine whether she is open or self-contained.

Does she show her feelings openly? Does she give a priority to relationships; use vocal inflections and animated facial and body expressions? Is her time perspective flexible? Are her decisions based more on emotions and feelings? If so, then she's more open. But if she's poker faced, keeps her distance physically and mentally, gives priority to tasks, disciplines her time, and makes decisions based more on logic and facts, she's more self-contained. Let's assume that your observation says she is self-contained; that eliminates the relater, so she is a cautious thinker.

Developing a Relationship Strategy to Match Your Customer's Behavior Style

Once you have determined your customer's style, you can start to treat your customer the way she wants to be treated. This often requires an adjustment in your behavior, specifically in your pace and priority. Because you can readily see whether the prospect is moving at a faster or slower pace than you, quickly make that adjustment. Then determine whether the prospect is focusing primarily on the *relationship* or the *task* and adjust accordingly.

Pace is the speed at which your customer prefers to operate. Those with direct styles (socializers and directors) prefer to move and decide quickly, whereas those with indirect styles (relaters and thinkers) prefer a slower, more cautious pace. If you go too fast for the indirect types, you will overrun their natural caution, but if you go too slow for the direct types, you will irritate and frustrate them.

Priority is the second area where you'll need to adjust your behavior. This refers to whether the prospect wants to focus on the relationship or the task at hand. The open styles (relaters and socializers) are relationship-oriented and will want to spend time getting to know you and letting you get to know them. The self-contained styles (directors and thinkers) will want to get down to the task immediately. Figure 6.4 summarizes how you can effectively modify your pace and priority.

Here's an overview of specific strategies that work with each style. Also, see Tables 6.3 and 6.4 for additional strategies to use in dealing effectively with each style.

Selling to directors
- Be prepared, organized, fast-paced, and always to the point.
- Meet them in a professional, businesslike manner.
- Find out their goals and motivations.
- Get to the point quickly, provide options, and let them make decisions when possible.
- To influence decisions, provide alternative actions with brief supporting analysis.
- If you disagree, argue facts, not personal feelings.
- Recognize their ideas—not them personally.
- Be punctual and don't waste their time.
- Above all else with the directors, *be efficient and competent.*

Selling to socializers
- Show them that you are interested in them as a person.
- Support their opinions, ideas, and dreams.
- Don't hurry the discussion.
- Try not to argue; you can seldom win.
- Let them talk; be enthusiastic and direct them toward mutually agreeable objectives.
- Provide testimonials and incentives to positively affect decisions.
- Summarize in writing the specifics of any agreement.
- Be entertaining and fast moving.
- Above all else with socializers, *be interested in them.*

Selling to relaters
- Get to know them personally.
- Be pleasant and friendly but professional and nonthreatening.
- Develop trust and credibility at a relatively slow pace.
- Assume that they'll take everything personally.

How to modify your pace and priority.

To Focus More on the Relationship:
- Share your feelings; let your emotions show.
- Respond to the expression of others' feelings.
- Pay personal compliments.
- Take time to develop the *relationship*.
- Use friendly language.
- Communicate more; loosen up and stand closer.
- Be willing to digress from the agenda; go with the flow.

To Focus More on the Task:
- Get right to the task, the bottom line, the business at hand.
- Maintain more of a logical, factual orientation.
- Keep to the agenda.
- Leave when the work is done; do not waste the other person's time.
- Do not initiate physical contact.
- Downplay your enthusiasm and body movement.
- Use businesslike language.

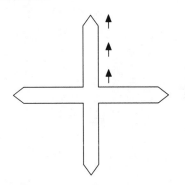

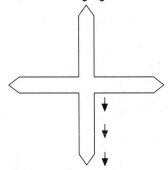

To Increase Your Pace:
- Speak and move at a faster pace.
- Initiate conversations and decisions.
- Give recommendations; don't ask for opinions.
- Use direct statements rather than roundabout questions.
- Communicate with a strong, confident voice.
- Challenge and tactfully disagree when appropriate.
- Face conflict openly, but don't conflict with your prospects.
- Increase your eye contact.

To Decrease Your Pace:
- Talk, walk, and make decisions more slowly.
- Seek and acknowledge the opinions of others.
- Share decision making and leadership.
- Show less energy; be more "mellow."
- Do not interrupt.
- When talking, provide pauses to give others a chance to speak.
- Refrain from criticizing, challenging, or acting pushy.
- When disagreeing, choose words carefully.

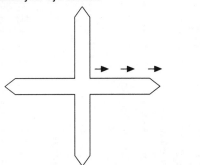

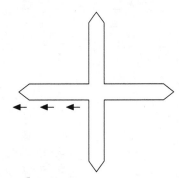

Figure 6.4 **How to modify your pace and priority.**

Table 6.3 Prescriptions for Flexibility

	Directors	Thinkers	Socializers	Relaters
Need to know about:	What it does/By when/What it costs	How they can justify it logically/How it works	How it enhances their status and visibility	How it will affect their personal circumstances
Do it with:	Conviction	Accuracy	Flair	Warmth
Save them:	Time	Embarrassment	Effort	Conflict
To facilitate decision making, provide:	Options with supporting analysis	Data and documentation	Testimonials and incentives	Personal service and assurances
Like you to be:	To the point	Precise	Stimulating	Pleasant
Support their:	Goals	Procedures	Ideas	Feelings
Create this environment:	Businesslike	Serious	Enthusiastic	Personal
Maintain this pace:	Fast/decisive	Slow/systematic	Fast/spontaneous	Slow/relaxed
Focus on this priority:	The task/The results	The task/The process	The relationship/Interaction	The relationship/Communication
At play be:	Competitive and aggressive	Structured/Play by the rules	Spontaneous and playful	Casual and cooperative
Use time to:	Act efficiently	Ensure accuracy	Enjoy the interaction	Develop the relationship
Write this way:	Short and to the point	Detailed and precise	Informal and dramatic	Warm and friendly
On the telephone be:	Short and to the point	Businesslike and precise	Conversational and playful	Warm and pleasant

- Ask them to explain their emotional needs as well as their task or business expectations.
- Get them involved by focusing on the human element.
- When you disagree, discuss personal feelings.
- Avoid rushing them and communicate with them on a consistent, regular basis.
- Show that you are actively listening.
- Provide guarantees and personal assurances that any actions will involve a minimum of risk.
- Above all else with relaters, *be warm and sincere.*

Selling to thinkers

- Be prepared and answer as many of their questions as soon as possible.
- Be systematic, exact, and organized.
- Proceed quickly to the task.
- Demonstrate through actions rather than words.
- Explain your logic and ask questions that reveal a clear direction.
- List advantages and disadvantages of any plan.
- Document how and why something applies.
- Provide solid, tangible, and factual evidence.
- Give them time to think and avoid pushing them.
- Provide guarantees that actions can't backfire.
- Follow through and deliver what you promise.
- Above all else with thinkers, *be thorough and well prepared.*

Summing Up

The key to success is to know who you're dealing with and to be able to adapt to that individual's needs. Worksheet 6.1 will help you develop a relationship strategies action plan to deal more effectively and appropriately with others. If you practice adjusting your selling style to fit the customer's buying style, you will create a situation where your customers are as eager to buy as you are to sell. At that point, you're ready to get into a serious exploration of their needs and concerns, which we'll address in the next section.

Table 6.4 **Selling by Style**

	Directors	**Thinkers**	**Socializers**	**Relaters**
Targeting:	Show that you've done your homework on their industry or company, and on them personally.	Bring logical proof that accurately documents your quality, track record, and value.	Show how your product can increase their social recognition and excitement while saving them effort.	Show how your product will stabilize, simplify, and support their existing practices and relationships.
Contacting:	Talk fast and in a businesslike manner. Focus on results, facts, and the bottom-line.	Speak slowly and accurately. Explain why you are contacting them.	Speak with friendly enthusiasm about aspirations and dreams. Let them set the conversational pace.	Relax and talk warmly and informally. Focus on feelings, relationships, and building trust.
Exploring:	Ask open and closed questions that focus on desired results and time constraints. Provide information about you while gathering information about them.	Ask open and closed questions that investigate their knowledge, systems, objectives, and objections. Make your questions short and crisp.	Ask open questions that explore their motivations, dreams, and expectations. Work business-related questions in with social questions.	Ask open questions that draw them out, especially around sensitive areas. Show tact and sincerity in probing about their work and relationship needs.

Collaborating:	Emphasize efficiency, profits, and savings. Present quick, concise analysis of their needs and your solutions.	Emphasize logic, accuracy, value, quality, and reliability. Present obvious disadvantages.	Emphasize uniqueness, innovativeness, excitement, visibility, and saving effort. Style of presentation as important as substance.	Emphasize security, harmony, steadiness, and company benefits. Involve them by asking for feedback.
Confirming:	Provide options with cost benefit summary of each. Acknowledge that the final decision is theirs.	Provide logical options with documentation. Give them enough time and data to analyze their options.	Act assumptive and quick. Use testimonials and incentives.	Make a mutual action plan. Provide personal guidance, direction, and assurance.
Assuring:	Provide ongoing reminders of your track record. Show them that you stand behind your product to deliver their results.	Set a specific timetable for when you'll measure success. Continue proving your reliability, quality, and value.	Save them effort and complications while making them look good. Check for proper product usage.	Practice consistent and predictable follow-up. Continue building your business relationship with personal attention and assistance.

WORKSHEET 6.1
Relationship Strategies Action Plan

1. My predominant behavioral style is: _____

2. Two people with whom I currently have a professional or social relationship are:

Person A: _____   Person B: _____

3. Based on my observations of each person's openness and directness, I would identify their behavioral styles as (director, thinker, socializer, or relater):

Person A's style: _____   Person B's style: _____

4. Two sources of stress in my relationship with each person are:

Person A:

     1. _____

     2. _____

Person B:

     1. _____

     2. _____

5. I would like to see my relationship with these two individuals improve in these specific ways or areas and for these reasons:

Person A:

Area 1: _____   Area 2: _____

Reasons or benefits to be gained: _____

_____

_____

Person B:

Area 1: _____   Area 2: _____

Reasons or benefits to be gained: _____

_____

_____

WORKSHEET 6.1 (continued)

6. These adjustments to my own behavioral style will demonstrate behavioral flexibility and work to accomplish improvements in my relationship with this person:

Adjustments I will make with Person A: _____

_____

_____

Adjustments I will make with Person B: _____

_____

_____

7. Because communication plays such a vital role in building and maintaining relationships, I plan to employ these three specific communication skills to assist me in achieving the improvements noted in Action Item 5:

With Person A, I will:

    1. _____

    2. _____

    3. _____

With Person B, I will:

    1. _____

    2. _____

    3. _____

8. Overall, taking into account my pace/priority adjustments *and* my conscious application of communication skills, the strategy that I will use as a foundation for building my relationship with each person will be:

Person A: _____

_____

Person B: _____

_____

STEP III

Exploring Your Customer's Needs

The exploring stage of sales gives you a chance to get deeply involved with your prospect to determine exactly how your product or service can help him. It's where the partnering process begins.

The purpose of exploring is to get enough information from the client to enable you to recommend appropriate options. But you have to do your homework first. Most salespeople do very little, if any, preparation before calling on the client. As a result, they ask poor questions that elicit minimal responses. Based on their incomplete picture of the client's situation, they make recommendations that may be totally inappropriate for the situation, and then they can't understand why the client is reluctant to buy.

In this section we're going to show you how to prepare thoroughly for your meeting with the client, including what questions to ask and how to ask them. We'll show you how to actively listen to the client and take meaningful notes that you and the client can use together to solve the problem or take advantage of an opportunity. Then, we'll show you how to handle the actual in-person sales call. Some of what we'll cover will take you "back to the basics." You may have heard some of these ideas before . . . but it's important to use them effectively on every call.

CHAPTER 7

Exploring Customer Needs Effectively by Asking the Right Questions

When we go into the field with salespeople from our client companies, we consistently find weaknesses in their ability to ask effective questions. We also find that they've been trained in this area but have not taken the time to apply what they've learned. We encourage you to make a commitment to master the skills included in the exploring stage of selling. These are the master skills of the successful salesperson, and they'll give you a lifetime competitive advantage.

How well do you explore with your customers? Please take a few moments now to complete Worksheet 7.1.

Research Your Target Company and Prospect

Effective questioning requires good research and preparation to maximize its potential. There are lots of valuable sources of information. Any good library will have dozens of reference materials. For publicly held companies, you can locate their annual reports and get more information from Standard & Poor's *Industry Surveys*. For smaller companies, check out *Contacts Influential*, a national compilation of sales leads offering marketing services such as lists, data bases, and so on. You'll also find criss-cross directories, which list addresses alphabetically with corresponding phone numbers in one half of the directory, and phone numbers numerically with corresponding addresses in the other half, and census reports for individual prospects. Your local business journal is also a good source of information. Many brokerage firms now sell information on publicly traded companies. Also check with your local chamber of commerce and local and national associations for your target industries.

Make friends with the reference librarians at your local library. They can help you find out almost anything you want to know. Talk to people

WORKSHEET 7.1
How Well Do I Explore with My Customers?

Circle the response that best corresponds to your behavior.

	Always	Sometimes	Never
1. I research all available sources to learn as much as I can about the prospect's company before contacting them.	___	___	___
2. Before each meeting I prepare a list of questions to ask my customer.	___	___	___
3. My list of questions covers appropriate standard topics, such as time/budget constraints, the decision-making process, current/desired situation, relevant past experiences, company politics, competitive exposure, and success criteria/expectations as well as topics specific to my products and services.	___	___	___
4. I use questions that elicit values, beliefs, and feelings rather than just facts.	___	___	___
5. I open with broad questions and move on to more specific questions later in the interview.	___	___	___
6. I use questions to expand, clarify, and redirect the conversation.	___	___	___
7. I listen actively and let the customer know I'm listening.	___	___	___
8. I summarize my customer's needs to clarify my understanding of the situation.	___	___	___
9. I ask my customer to prioritize the needs we mutually agreed on.	___	___	___
10. I work with my customer to come up with success criteria.	___	___	___

who *use* your prospect's product. Talk to his competitor's customers. After all, you're trying to help your prospect be more competitive, aren't you? Learn his industry so you can speak his language. Worksheet 7.2 is designed to help you prepare for meeting with your prospect.

Develop a Questioning Plan

After you've researched your prospect, it's time to develop your questioning plan. You'll need to think through everything you need to know to fully understand your client's situation so you can make an appropriate, workable recommendation. Then develop a list of questions that will get you the information you'll need. That way you can concentrate on listening to your client's responses instead of trying to think up your next question.

In traditional selling, we were taught that the truly great salesperson went into the client's office like John Wayne and wrestled the client into submission with his bare hands. It was a display of raw power. Certainly, that model of selling left no room for thoughtful preparation . . . and there was no way that John Wayne would ever show up with a list of questions! Are you kidding?

To bring you back to reality, put yourself in the customer's shoes. Imagine that you are thinking about remodeling your home. Being a smart consumer, you decide to have at least two contractors submit bids. The first one comes to your home, looks around your house, and asks you a few questions like, "How old is the house?" "What areas do you want to remodel?" "Will you need financing?" "How much equity do you have in the house?" "When do you want to start and when do you need it finished?" He then pulls out a contract, fills in several blanks, puts a price on it, and asks you to sign on the bottom line.

The second contractor comes in with a sketch pad. On a separate pad she has a list of questions. Her questions include: "Could you tell me a little bit about what's prompting this project?" "In what area of your home do you spend the most time?" "What area of your home is your favorite and why?" "Which area is your least favorite and why?" As you discuss each area of your home, she takes detailed notes and then asks for a thorough tour. She sketches, measures, and listens as you talk about your concerns and deadlines. Before she leaves, she reviews her notes to make sure she hasn't forgotten anything. She asks you if it would be all right if she goes back to the office and prepares a plan, a schedule, and a budget for your project. When you say yes, she requests a meeting with you in two

WORKSHEET 7.2
Preparing to Explore

For this worksheet, use whatever sources are available to you to gather information about major issues in your target company and its industry.

1. Choose a company from your target market of potential customers:

_____

2. Investigate as many of the following sources as you can for the company you've chosen:

    - Sales and earnings last year
    - Major competitors
    - Major products

    - Number of people and locations
    - Recent trends in their industry

    - Company mission or vision
    - Annual report/K-10 report
    - Associations decision makers belong to
    - Stock symbol

    - Recent stock activity

    - Trade journals your prospect might read
    - Recent national/state/local issues affecting the business
    - Current financial position—is the trend up or down?
    - Names, addresses, and phone numbers of key decision makers

3. Now, using the information you've gathered, develop a competitive advantage statement you could use in an initial contact with this company:

_____

_____

4. Based on what you've learned, what benefits related to your product or service do you feel this company would be seeking?

_____

_____

_____

WORKSHEET 7.2 (continued)

5. Does this company fit the profile of your best customers? Why or why not?

    _____

    _____

6. Who should you call on in this company? Who will be the key decision maker?

    _____

    _____

days to discuss her ideas. Which contractor has your interest, your confidence, your trust? On the basis of this first meeting, which contractor would you tend to hire?

Ask Open-Ended Questions

There are two big differences between the traditional contractor's method of fact-finding and the second contractor's method of exploring. One is the way the question is phrased, and the other is the content of the response you are seeking. Fact-finding questions are typically closed-ended questions that can be answered with a yes, a no, or a one-word answer, whereas exploring questions are typically open-ended questions.

Examples of closed-ended questions include, "How long have you been in business?" "How many bedrooms are you looking for in a home?" "Are you happy with your current computers?" Examples of open-ended questions are "Could you tell me a little about your company?" "How would you describe your current personal investment strategy?" "Tell me what's important to you in a home security system."

The more significant difference between fact-finding and exploring is in the *content* of the response you are seeking. If your question seeks only to uncover raw data—facts—then it's a fact-finding question. While there's nothing wrong with those questions at the right time, they don't really give you much information about your prospect and his motivations.

On the other hand, if you are trying to discover your customer's priorities, values, goals, ideas, view of the future, feelings, internal political concerns, financial situation, and so on, then you are exploring!

Fact-finding questions that only seek raw data include:

- "How many computer work stations do you have now?"
- "How many people need to use them ?"
- "Do you own or lease?"

Fact-finding questions bore the client. Almost every computer salesperson asks those same questions . . . the prospect has probably heard them a hundred times. The minute you ask this type of question, the prospect puts you into the "just another computer salesperson" category and stops listening.

Exploring questions, on the other hand, sound like this:

- "How do your people feel about your current work station setup?"
- "What problems do they have getting access to a computer when they need one?"
- "In your view, what impact has the shortage had on productivity?"
- "What factors prompted your decision to own or lease?"

Solve Your Customer's Problems

Whenever you work with a customer, you should always be looking for problems . . . and opportunities. The only two ways you can help your customer are to *solve a problem* for him or to help him *take advantage of a new opportunity*. Problems are things he wants to *move away from* and opportunities are the things he wants to *move toward*.

Most people have a dominant pattern of consistently moving away from problems or toward opportunities. If you can identify your prospect's pattern, you can position your product to meet his specific need by *reflecting their language* about the problem or opportunity. People who move away from problems are motivated primarily by a fear of something. These people tend to be the thinkers and relaters we profiled in Chapter 6. People who move toward opportunities are motivated primarily by a desire for something. These people tend to be the directors and socializers.

For instance, imagine that you're talking with an advertising agency about a new computer. The decision maker says she would like to have a new computer, but she can't buy one now because business is slow. You ask what she believes is causing the problem, and she tells you she feels that she's lost touch with her clients. You ask what action she's taken; she says none. She's considered several alternatives but rejected them all. Her pattern is to move away. She is motivated by fear.

So you ask her if she's ever thought of doing a newsletter and she says, "Yes, but it seemed too complex and time-consuming." Her approach continues to be to move away from problems.

If, after you've finished exploring her situation, you could show her how she could move away from her problems of slow business and lost customer contact by using your computer's easy-to-learn, easy-to-use, problem-free desktop publishing system, you will have solved her problem of lost contact. If you can also show her how she can solve the cash flow problem with your easy payment plan that includes low monthly payments and no payment at all for the first 90 days, you will have solved her financing problem . . . and gotten a sale. You've also found out a lot about her business, and you've started to form a strong business relationship. You're not just trying to sell her something . . . you're trying to help her be more successful in her business.

Build Relationships with Your Customers

Exploring questions challenge your customer to think more deeply about her situation and how it might be improved. They get her involved in the problem-solving process, and it's much more fun, creative work for your client than just responding with facts. Exploring is part of the process of *building a relationship.* You want to paint a *complete* picture of the customer's situation, not just the little corner that deals with her computer needs. You need to see your product in the context of her larger problem or opportunity. You want to find out her values and priorities . . . how she feels about the product or service. You're looking for a total solution, not just a computer solution.

Many salespeople think that it's a waste of time to learn everything about a prospect's business when you only want to sell him a computer. They believe that you should just tell the prospect how great your computer is and ask for his order. That approach might be okay if you happened to walk in the day the prospect's current computer died. But that's not normally the case. Usually, one of two things happens. Either you approach a prospect who is perfectly happy with his current computer system, or you approach a prospect who isn't happy with his current system but is already talking to your competition.

If he's happy with his current computer, you'll need to ask some questions that start him thinking about its shortcomings or about the possibilities he's missing by not having state-of-the-art equipment. If he's not happy with his computer system but he's already talking to your competition, you'll need to know more about his situation, values, feelings, and priorities than your prospect does if you're going to come up with the most appropriate solution.

Recognize Your Customer's Priorities

One of the biggest reasons sales are lost is because of a poor understanding of the customer's *priorities*. How many times have you proposed the perfect solution to a significant problem only to have the customer tell you that while you did a great job, it just isn't a priority right now, or that they just don't have the budget, or that the boss changed his mind? These are priority problems. Computers (or cars or overnight delivery or advertising services) may be important, maybe even critical, but if your customer has a higher priority, it's no sale. That's why understanding the complete picture is so important. It gives you the information you need to align your product or service within the customer's overall priorities.

If you ask a prospect only fact-finding questions, generally you'll quickly discover he's not interested . . . not a qualified prospect. You'll turn around, walk away, and take his name off your prospect list. But if you talk to him about his business and start to gather information about the problems he's facing—his challenges—you may uncover an opportunity. You might find out that he's losing sales by not having detailed information about inventory levels, something your whiz-bang computer will do easily for him. By finding out what his needs and expectations are, you let him know you are interested in him. You're beginning to build trust. In the end you may even find out he doesn't need your computer. He might have the oldest, slowest computer in the world, but it's meeting his needs perfectly. You may walk away without a sale, but you'll still have a relationship. And someday, when that old, slow computer dies completely, the prospect will think of you because you were interested in him and his priorities.

How to Explore Your Customer's Needs

Another signal that you need to do more exploring is when you find yourself getting a lot of objections at the end of your sales process. You get those objections because you're not doing enough exploring up front to truly understand your customer's situation. As you develop your list of questions, you'll need to think about the steps we'll list here plus whatever special information you'll need concerning your specific product.

1. Explore your prospect's *current situation*

- Exactly what business is she in and where are the profits generated?
- Who are her customers?
- What are the problems and challenges facing her?
- What's happening in her industry?
- What's changing?
- What is the organization structure?

2. Explore your prospect's *desired situation*

- What would she like to have happen?
- Where would she like to see improvement?
- What would that improvement mean to her or her company?
- What are her goals and visions for her company?
- What are her personal goals?
- What concerns does she have about the future?
- What problems does she foresee?

3. Explore your prospect's experience with previous products   After you've explored the customer's current situation and desired situation, you move on to *relevant past experiences.* Pay special attention to negative past experiences. Has the customer had any recent experiences that have colored her thinking, such as product failures, personality conflicts, or service problems? Few sales situations are as difficult as confronting a prospect who has a chip on her shoulder from a past injustice. The best thing to do is listen to the client and assure her you will do everything in your power to see that her bad experience is rectified and never repeated. Also, exceptionally good experiences with other competitors could make your customer favor another vendor.

4. Identify your prospect's "need gap"   The difference between the prospect's current situation and desired situation is the need gap. The smaller the need gap, the less likely the prospect will take any action. The larger the need gap, the greater the desire to take immediate action to rectify—or close—it.

After analyzing a prospect's situation, if you find his need gap to be too small or nonexistent, then your product or service may offer little or no improvement. In this case, you would advise the client not to buy. When this happens, wrap up the call so you will not waste either your time or his. You might wrap things up by saying something like, "Mr. Jones, based on what we've discussed, it looks like I can't offer you a way to improve your sales. If, in the next six months, however, you find your sales do not grow by more than 5 percent [or some other condition], we would have a basis for doing business. Do you mind if I keep in touch to see how your sales are progressing?"

When you recontact him, ask how things are in general, and then ask questions to see if those specific conditions have changed. If they have not, ask if you can call back again in three to six months. If they have changed, get together and look at his situation again.

5. Initiate decision making   Let's assume that the initial phase of exploration has yielded good results. The message is: "Let's continue talking." Now you'll need to explore the *decision-making process:*

- How does the decision-making process work?
- How long is a normal decision process?
- Are there any deadlines involved?

6. Establish *decision criteria*

- What criteria will be used to determine the company and the product or service that is chosen?
- What are the customer's expectations?
- What is the relative value of each criterion?

7. Determine the *decision makers*

- Who will be involved in the decision-making process?
- Will the decision makers consult any outside experts or authorities?
- Do some decision makers carry more weight than others—like the husband or the wife or the CPA?

- Does anyone have veto power?
- What role will each play?

In business-to-business sales, often the person who *places the order* isn't the person who *makes the decision*. So when you interact with a company, it is essential to analyze the roles of the different people in the decision-making process. Some of these roles will overlap, but for the most part, they are divided into 6 types:

1. The *initiator* is the person who first suggests or thinks of buying a particular product or service.
2. The *gatekeeper* is a person, usually a secretary or receptionist, who has control over the accessibility of someone you wish to speak to or see.
3. The *influencer* is someone who's part of the decision-making process whose opinion or advice weighs heavily in the final decision.
4. The *decision maker* is obviously the person who is responsible for the ultimate decision of what to buy, how many, when, and from whom.
5. The *buyer* is the person who actually makes the purchase.
6. The *user* is the consumer or person who is employing the product or service regularly.

In our computer example the roles might be as follows:

- The initiator would be the chief financial officer.
- The gatekeepers would be several secretaries and receptionists.
- The influencers would be the accounting staff and service technicians.
- The decision maker would be the CEO.
- The buyer would be the head of purchasing.
- The users would be the staffs of various departments.

Knowing how these roles impact the sales process can help you plan an effective strategy for winning the account.

In a complex situation like this, try to find an inside coach. As your ally, that person can guide you through the organization, provide you with key information, and introduce you to other decision makers.

And don't forget *politics*:

- Are there any hidden agendas that you need to know about?
- Do others in the organization or the household stand to gain or lose as a result of the final decision?

■ Are there any special loyalties to other companies, other salespeople, or specific product brands?

Politics or conflicts within an organization can often derail even a perfect sales plan. Asking about politics and agendas up-front can often reveal potential pitfalls and give you a chance to develop a strategy to handle them.

8. Investigate your *competitive exposure*

■ What other companies are being considered?
■ Is the customer currently working with your competitors?
■ What do they particularly like or dislike about the competition's offerings?

9. Establish *success criteria and expectations*

■ After the purchase, how will the client specifically measure the success of your product or service?
■ Will this purchase impact his performance-measurement process?
■ Are there specific quality standards that must be met?

The reason you must ask these questions is that they will provide a concrete basis on which to measure the efficacy of your product or service after the sale. To accurately track performance, you need to have success criteria that are realistic, specific, and measurable.

10. Assess your customer's *buying urgency*

In exploring, it may be important for you to know how quickly a prospect will want to act if the sale were to be confirmed. The time factor gives you a lot of insight. A prospect who recognizes a need but is in no hurry to change may be doing one of two things: either taking bids from competitors or gathering as much information as possible. It will be important for you to know which.

The urgency of the purchase will also impact your ability to deliver on promises. If there is some doubt as to the speed with which you can deliver, you will have to be a liaison between your prospect and your company. Go back to your company and see if you can convince them to rush the order if it comes through. This difficult balancing act is part of being a consultant representing the desires and limitations of two parties—the customer and the company. This is known as upstream and downstream selling. An example of this is seen in the insurance industry. An insurance salesperson has to sell you first (downstream selling) and then go back to her company and sell the underwriting department on your being a safe bet to insure (upstream selling).

11. Finally, consider *budget constraints*

- Is a budget already committed to the project?
- How will the financial decision be made—by return on investment? Payback period? Cost savings?
- Will financing be needed?
- Who will provide it?

Summing Up

You should examine all of the areas discussed in this chapter to create an exploration plan that makes sense for your prospect. Of course, this is a general guide; your prospect's unique situation may send you down an entirely different path. But by thinking through the situation in advance, you'll be prepared to be flexible. Preparation is a major part of exploring, and it can yield big dividends when done well.

Once you've asked your clients the right questions, you need to know how to listen to the answers. The next chapter will give you a guide for listening to not only what your prospects say, but what they don't say. Active listening will give you the tools to make sense of all the information you've gathered from your prospects.

CHAPTER 8

Listening Actively to Your Customers

You've prepared a list of very important questions. Now it's important to focus on the specifics of how to be an effective listener. When we think of a successful salesperson, we often think of a talker . . . someone who has the gift of gab . . . someone whose way with words convinces people to buy even if they aren't interested in the product or service. This talker-salesperson starts telling the prospect about his product before he even knows what the prospect needs or wants. That's what we refer to as prescription *before* diagnosis . . . and that's malpractice. Studies of the very best salespeople show that it's their listening skills, not their persuasive talking skills, that distinguish them from average performers.

Ineffective listening is one of the most frequent causes of:

- Misunderstandings
- Mistakes
- Jobs that need to be redone
- Lost sales and customers

If all of these negatives result from ineffective listening, why don't we listen more effectively? Here are several reasons:

Listening is hard work   Listening is more than just keeping quiet. An *active* listener registers increased blood pressure, a higher pulse rate, and more perspiration. It means concentrating on the other person rather than on yourself. As a result, a lot of people just don't do it.

Information overload screens things out   In today's society there is enormous competition for our attention from advertisements, radio, TV, movies, reading material, and more. With all these incoming stimuli, we have learned to screen out information that we deem irrelevant. Sometimes we also screen out things that are important to us.

Impatience causes a rush to action   We want action. We think we know what a person is going to say, so we jump in and interrupt rather than take the necessary time to listen and hear the person out.

Speed of speech differs from speed of thought   There is a considerable difference between speech speed and thought speed. The average person speaks at about 135 to 175 words a minute but can listen to 400 to 500 words a minute. So, while someone else is talking, the listener can also daydream . . . or think of what he is going to say next . . . or mentally argue with the person speaking. It's like listening to two voices at the same time.

Lack of training   We do more listening than speaking, reading, or writing, yet we receive almost no formal education in listening. In fact, in the first 12 years of schooling the average student gets less than half a year of listening instruction!

How Active Listening Benefits Sales

Listening well—listening actively—is obviously important, but how does it really benefit you? Listening well has the following benefits:

- It improves the environment at work, at home, and in sales.
- It reduces relationship tensions and hostilities.
- It saves time by reducing mistakes and misunderstandings.
- It leads to early problem solving.
- It increases sales and profits.

Let's start by defining listening as the process of receiving a message the way the customer intended to send it. Note that an untrained listener misses as much as 50% of the message, and reflect on how that could affect the sales process. Every time a customer says, "I didn't understand," or "Is that what you meant?" or "I didn't hear you say that," or "We had a misunderstanding due to poor communication," it's because the salesperson didn't practice good listening skills.

There are three levels of listening: *marginal listening, evaluative listening,* and *active listening.*

Marginal listening   This is the lowest level of listening; it involves the least concentration. A listener in this state displays blank stares or nervous mannerisms. The salesperson is distracted by surroundings and his own thoughts. Any salesperson who's listening at this level is in deep trouble. The prospect will feel your lack of attention, be insulted, and lose trust in you. For example, a prospect looking at a copy machine might say, "I'm not sure it's big enough to handle my needs." The marginally listening salesperson responds, "We offer a three-year warranty with each machine." The salesperson is running through a spiel and not connecting with the information the customer is offering.

Evaluative listening   This is at the next level of listening: Here, the salesperson is paying attention and concentrating somewhat. The salesperson hears the words but not the intent. In evaluative listening, the salesperson leaps ahead to what he thinks the message is going to be and prepares an answer before the customer is even finished with her statement. When the customer states a concern about the size of the copy machine, the evaluatively listening salesperson hears the concern about size and leaps into a canned response: "We have copiers that can handle any copy volume." He makes an assumption about the customer's concern and responds in a way that may not be appropriate. Neither marginal listening nor evaluative listening is sufficient to give you a competitive advantage.

Active listening   This is the third and most effective level of listening. The active listener refrains from evaluating the message and tries to see the prospect's point of view, paying attention not only to the words spoken, but to the thoughts and ideas as well . . . the intent. When our copying machine prospect makes the statement about it being big enough to meet her needs, the actively listening salesperson says, "Tell me more about what you need in a copy machine."

The salesperson defers his judgment *and* the sales presentation until he knows more about the customer's needs. He is trying to get past the words to find out the real concern behind the prospect's statement. Behind the words are a lot of thoughts and feelings—our prospect may be concerned about the copier capacity, or perhaps about speed. She may also just be talking about physical size and wondering if the machine will fit in the space she has in mind for it!

Active listeners listen *behind* the words for the *thoughts and feelings*, but they also listen *between* the words for what is *not* being said. Sometimes customers reveal much more by what they don't say. There are several ways to hear the emotions behind the words. First, look for changes in eye contact. After you have established a comfortable and natural level of eye contact, any sudden deviations will tip you off to emotional content in the message. People tend to look away from you when they talk about something embarrassing. When this happens, make a quick mental note of what subject caused the embarrassment, and treat that subject delicately. You should also give your prospect the courtesy of looking away momentarily yourself, as if you are saying, "I respect your privacy."

How to Become an Active Listener

These five steps, when followed, will help you become an active listener:

1. Concentrate by focusing your attention on the customer and only on the customer.
2. Acknowledge your customer by demonstrating your interest and attention.
3. Research—gather information about your customer through the skillful use of questions and statements.
4. Sense the nonverbal messages of your customer by observing what he's saying with his body language.
5. Structure or organize the information you get through your listening, observation, and note taking.

Each of these steps is described in detail, but before you begin working to improve your listening skills, let's first look at where you are at this moment in each of the key areas of effective listening.

How to Assess Your Listening Skills

Take a few minutes to respond to the questions in Worksheet 8.1, "Listening Skills Assessment." Your responses will help you determine what specific skills need improvement. Respond *honestly* to each of the items—no one is going to review or use this survey but you.

Now that you have responded to the items in Worksheet 8.1, you have a road map for improving your listening skills. Any item marked as "Sometimes" or "Never" identifies a listening skill that needs improvement. For any item you marked as "Always," congratulations!

Step 1: Concentrate on What Your Customer Is Saying

Now let's talk about the specifics of how to be a better active listener. The first technique is to *concentrate*, to clear the distractions around you when-

WORKSHEET 8.1
Listening Skills Assessment

Circle the appropriate response.

	Always	Sometimes	Never

Concentration Skills

1. When I talk with others, my mind is completely absorbed by what they are saying and it seldom wanders.

2. When in a conversation with others, I hold my comments until others are finished talking, even though my comments may have direct relevance to what they are saying at that moment.

3. I do not let distractions like ringing telephones, busy street traffic, or other conversations in a room distract my attention from what someone is saying to me.

Acknowledgment Skills

4. When talking face-to-face or on the phone with someone, I acknowledge what is being said with "I understand" or "I see" or other comments that let the customer know I'm listening.

Research Skills

5. Whenever I talk with someone, I encourage the conversation and ensure that it will be a two-way flow of communication by asking open-ended questions, clarifying what I don't completely understand, and giving appropriate feedback.

WORKSHEET 8.1 (continued)

	Always	Sometimes	Never
6. I let others know that I am listening and trying to understand what they say by using phrases like, "Tell me more about that," or, "Can you give me an example?" or "Then what?"	___	___	___

Sensing Skills

7. When I am talking with others, I read their body language as well as listen to their words, to fully interpret what they are telling me.	___	___	___
8. When talking with others, I try to read what's going on behind their spoken words by asking myself what they might be feeling, why they are saying what they are saying, and what is *implied* by what they say.	___	___	___

Structuring Skills

9. Whenever I talk with others, I take either mental or written notes of the major idea, the key points, and the supporting points and/or reasons.	___	___	___
10. As I take my mental or written notes, I sequence—I listen for order or priority.	___	___	___

ever possible—ringing telephones, high noise levels, and interruptions. You also need to clear your internal distractions—concerns about your family or upcoming deadlines, anything that might keep you from devoting 100% of your attention to the customer. All of those worries or distractions will still be waiting for you once you're finished with the customer. It is also important not to interrupt the customer or try to rush him.

To become an active listener, then, you must concentrate completely on the customer. As the salesperson, you must eliminate as many distractions as possible when listening to others. All distractions create enormous barriers that prevent the message from getting from the customer to you, the listener.

Here are some ways you can better concentrate on your customer.

Create a receptive listening environment   Such an environment is as devoid as possible of any audio or visual distractions. Try to provide a private, quiet, comfortable setting, especially in terms of temperature and seating. If you're meeting at the customer's place of business, you have less control over the external environment, but if there are a lot of distractions, such as ringing phones or frequent interruptions, you can recommend moving into a meeting room with more privacy. If that's not possible, suggest a later meeting in a more receptive listening environment in neutral territory such as a quiet, out-of-the-way restaurant.

Avoid violating another person's personal space   Some people are contact-oriented whereas others are noncontact-oriented. When you're talking with people, keep in mind that some may be very open and like to communicate in close proximity to you, while others may tend to be more self-contained and want to keep a greater physical distance.

Contact-oriented people tend to sit much closer to those with whom they are speaking. They communicate much closer as well, and they even touch when they communicate. This is quite common in some cultural backgrounds, such as Italian, Arab, Greek, French, Latin American, and several of the Mediterranean cultures. Examples of noncontact cultures include the Japanese, German, English, and to some degree American.

Focus on what your customer is saying   When distractions can't be avoided, minimize them by focusing and concentrating totally on the customer. Use the following four techniques of applied concentration to help you focus and concentrate on the customer:

- *Mentally paraphrase what the customer is saying.* Mentally paraphrasing what the customer is saying will prevent you from daydreaming or thinking of irrelevant and superfluous topics, especially if the customer to whom you are listening speaks slowly. Try to echo, rephrase, evaluate, anticipate, and review what the customer is saying so that you focus and concentrate on the customer instead of yourself.

- *Visually observe the other person.* Keep in mind the hitchhiking theory: where your eyes focus, your ears will follow. You are most likely to listen to what you are looking at. Make direct eye contact for several seconds before looking away. Prolonged eye contact may convey either intimidation or intimacy.
- *Eliminate, or at least diminish, all distractions.*
- *Focus your attention solely and directly on the person speaking.*

Concentrating completely on the person speaking to you especially requires the last two techniques.

Step 2: Acknowledge that You Are Listening to Your Customer

In the context of active listening, *acknowledging* means that salespeople give positive, observable, and frequently audible signs to the customer that they are listening to, understanding, and appreciating what the customer says. As an active listener, your acknowledgment communicates an attitude of acceptance of the customer as a worthwhile person. On the other hand, nonacknowledging or negative acknowledging demonstrated by the poor listener communicates disapproval and rejection and weakens the relationship between the customer and the salesperson. The result of such poor acknowledging is an interruption or an end to the communication process.

Think again of that person with whom you enjoy sharing conversations. From the two lists below, determine which group, the left or the right, contains the words that describe the body language and gestures of the person who shows an interest in you and what you are saying.

■ Glances sideways	■ Looks in your eyes
■ Sighs	■ Touches your arm or hand
■ Crosses arms on chest	■ Leans toward you
■ Leans away from you	■ Smiles frequently
■ Stares	■ Maintains a pleasant facial expression
■ Sneers	■ Grins
■ Yawns	■ Sits so as to face you directly
■ Frowns	■ Nods head affirmatively as you speak
■ Looks at the ceiling	■ Licks lips
■ Shakes head negatively	■ Raises eyebrows
■ Cleans fingernails	■ Keeps eyes wide open
■ Cracks knuckles	■ Uses expressive hand gestures while speaking
■ Jingles change or rattles keys	■ Gives fast glances
■ Fidgets in chair	■ Stretches

The gestures on the left-hand list usually make us feel like someone isn't very interested in what we're saying, whereas the right-hand list contains many of the gestures people use to let us know they're listening. In addition to the nonverbal acknowledgment, an active listener acknowledges the customer verbally as well with such comments as "I see," "Uh-huh," "Then what?" "Mmmm," or "Really?" Even the empathic comments such as "I don't believe it!" show the customer that you're alert, you're listening, and you care.

When acknowledging your customer both verbally and nonverbally, you accomplish many things that build trust and increase the customer's comfort level. Through your acknowledgment, the customer knows that:

- You are *listening*.
- Understand the *content* of what is being said.
- You understand how he/she *feels*.
- You understand the essential *meaning* of what is being said.
- You are *interested* in him or her and what is said.

Step 3: Research Your Customer's Ideas by Asking the Right Questions

As an active listener, *researching* is what you do to keep a conversation a two-way communication. It requires the information-gathering techniques of questioning and feedback. It enables you to clarify what you've heard, enlarge upon a subject, or explore a particular topic in more depth. Researching allows you to encourage the customer to change the direction of the conversation or prompt the customer to "vent" such feelings as anger, excitement, and enthusiasm. It also allows you to support and reinforce particular points that he has said to you.

The person who doesn't *actively* participate in the conversation through questions and feedback will make the customer feel uncomfortable by creating an information imbalance. Such an imbalance occurs when one person does all the talking and provides all the information while the other person simply listens—or *appears* to listen. Eventually the customer becomes concerned that the salesperson knows a lot about him but he doesn't know *anything* about the salesperson. Such a situation can make the customer feel tense and suspicious.

Your ability to ask the right questions at the right time while responding with appropriate feedback are essential and integral parts of the skill of researching. We already covered the art of asking questions, so let's focus more on the effective use of feedback.

Feedback is the other important aspect of researching if you want a conversation to continue for any length of time. Without giving feedback, how does the salesperson really know what the customer is trying to communicate? The effective use of feedback helps ensure that you receive an accurate message.

You use feedback whenever you react verbally, vocally, or visibly to what another person says or does. Active listening depends on it.

As a listener, you give feedback in several ways. You give verbal feedback, nonverbal feedback (as we discussed in the acknowledgment section), and feeling feedback. Each serves a specific purpose in active listening.

Giving verbal feedback   Verbal feedback is what you use most often. You use it to give and to ask for clarification of what the customer said and to encourage the customer to continue. In clarifying that you understood what was said, reflect back to the customer your understanding of her words. Note that we said "reflect back" rather than "*repeat* back." In other words, be sure that you use *your own words*; otherwise you will simply be parroting the customer instead of demonstrating your understanding of what was said.

For example, suppose your customer says, "The last copier I bought was always down or having to be serviced." You might respond in one of two ways: If you say, "The last copier you bought had a lot of service problems," this is merely *parroting* your customer's concern. On the other hand, if you say, "You seem to be afraid that a new copier might have lots of downtime and service problems," this is an example of *verbal feedback*. As for clarifying to improve your understanding of what was said, you can use such phrases as:

"I get the impression that you feel . . ."
"I sense that . . ."
"It sounds like you . . ."
"In other words, . . ."
"What I'm hearing is . . ."

Be sure to vary your introductory words when clarifying what has been said, or else it will appear as though you're really not listening but simply following a script.

Verbal feedback can also take the form of broad questions and the appropriate follow-up questions built on the customer's responses that we discussed earlier.

Giving nonverbal feedback   Projecting positive nonverbal feedback to the customer through gestures and utterances lets the customer know that her message is getting through to you. People want feedback; they need feedback. They don't like to talk with people who don't respond or show any emotion.

Feeling feedback   Obviously a firm understanding of the words, phrases, and facts of a message is important. However, that still represents just surface understanding. To truly understand your customer's needs, you need to know:

- Why is the person saying the things she is saying?
- What are the underlying causes and motivations behind her message?
- How does she really feel about what she is saying to you?
- Does she know whether her message is really getting through to you—at the feeling level?
- Is she aware that you really care about what she is saying to you?

All these questions underscore the importance of *feeling* feedback in active listening. Feeling feedback should be two-directional. You need to make a concerted effort to *understand* the feelings, emotions, and attitudes that underlie the message that comes to you. In addition, you should clearly *project feeling feedback* to the other person to demonstrate that her message has gotten through to you—at the feeling level.

Feeling feedback is a meeting of the hearts. It is nothing more than the effective use of empathy—putting yourself into the other person's shoes so that you can see things from her point of view. When you can really experience the other person's true feelings and understand where she's coming from and at the same time project this emotional awareness to her, it serves to reinforce rapport, lower interpersonal tension, and significantly increase trust. Supportive and understanding responses and an awareness and projection of appropriate nonverbal signals are the key tools used in sending and receiving feeling feedback.

When listening to someone, try to read the primary feeling the customer is projecting and respond to that feeling, allowing then for the customer to agree or to correct your "reading." For example:

Salesperson: You seem to be somewhat distressed about the service you've received.
Customer: Somewhat distressed? Are you kidding? I'm very angry about the mismanagement of the entire situation!

Another technique that is excellent for getting people to respond and share their feelings and thoughts with you is the use of empathy statements. Empathy statements consist of three specific parts:

1. A tentative statement
2. Defining the feeling
3. Putting the feeling into its situational context

An example of such an empathy statement is:

"It seems to me that you're very frustrated because you can't get the product to work the way you want it to."

The phrase "It seems to me" is the tentative statement. The phrase "you're very frustrated" defines the feeling, and the phrase "because you can't get the product to work the way you want it to" is putting the feeling into its situational context—the situation that caused the customer to experience the feeling of frustration.

Step 4: Sense Your Customer's Message by Interpreting Nonverbal Communication

Sensing refers to the ability to perceive messages sent *vocally* and *visually* as well as verbally. We respond to the gestures of others based on a preconscious understanding of the "secret" code of nonverbal communication—the vocal and visual messages sent by those speaking.

Watch for body language   The concept of body language—the visual part of nonverbal communication—is certainly not new. People have known about it and have used it since the beginning of time. Before people developed language as a communication tool, they used body language to make their needs and desires known to others. Also known as kinesics, body language describes human interaction beyond the use of written and spoken words.

Some nonverbal gestures represent universal symbolism. The chair at the head of the table has long been reserved for the leader of the group. More recently, this position of honor has also been extended to the host of the table. Another universal gesture is raising the hands above the head, which has long symbolized surrender and submission.

Some gestures are even more expressive than words. Conjure up the image of a person slapping his forehead. This may be accompanied by an audible groan. Don't you already know that he has remembered something he was supposed to do? Implicit in this gesture is a rebuke to himself for his oversight. Other well-known gestures are saluting, tipping one's hat, shaking hands, shrugging shoulders, waving good-bye, forming an "O" with thumb and forefinger, and blowing a kiss.

Body language involves the salesperson's interpretation of many kinds of gestures made by the customer's eyes, face, hands, arms, legs, and posture. You can glean a considerable amount of information about others, and they about you, simply by noting body gestures. However, each isolated gesture is like an isolated word in a sentence; it is very difficult and dangerous to interpret the gesture by itself or out of context. Unless it's a one-word sentence, it takes more than one gesture to provide full meaning. Consequently, you should consider the gesture in light of everything else that's going on around you.

Interpreting *gesture clusters* ensures a more meaningful analysis of the customer's state of mind, if these clusters are in harmony with the other messages the customer is sending. In other words, all the individual gestures must fit together to project a common, unified message. When they do not, you are faced with incongruity. A good example of incongruity is nervous laughter. Remember that body language can augment, emphasize, or even contradict the words that someone is speaking.

Let's examine some of the more common gesture clusters and their associated meanings.

- *Openness:* Several gestures indicate openness and sincerity, such as open hands, an unbuttoned coat or unbuttoned collar, removing a coat or jacket, moving closer to someone else, leaning slightly forward in one's chair, and uncrossed arms and legs.
- *Defensiveness:* On the other hand, defensiveness is usually projected by a rigid body, rigid or tightly crossed arms or legs, eyes glancing sideways or darting occasionally, minimal eye contact, pursed lips, clenched fists, and a downcast head. Be especially aware of tightly clenched fists—they show that the other person is really turned off.
- *Evaluation:* Evaluation gestures suggest that the other person is considering what you are saying—sometimes in a friendly way, sometimes unfriendly. Typical evaluation gestures include a tilted head, touching a hand to the cheek, leaning forward, and stroking the chin. Sometimes evaluation gestures take on a critical aspect. In this case, the body is usually more drawn back, the hand is to

the face, and the chin is in the palm of the hand with one finger going up the cheek and the other fingers positioned below the mouth.

■ *Self-conflict:* A person usually expresses this by pinching the bridge of the nose or closing the eyes, and slumping the head down slightly. He is probably trying to decide if he's in a bad situation or not. Don't try to reason him out of it; give him time.

■ *Negative evaluation:* A person dropping his or her eyeglasses to the lower bridge of the nose and peering over them is projecting a negative evaluation. Suspicion, secrecy, rejection, and doubt are typically communicated by sideways glances, minimal or no eye contact, shifting the body away from the other person, and touching or rubbing the bridge of the nose quite frequently.

■ *Readiness:* This is another cluster that communicates dedication to a goal. A person usually communicates it by placing the hands on the hips or sitting forward at the edge of a chair.

■ *Boredom, impatience:* These are usually conveyed by drumming the fingers, cupping the head in the palm of the hand, swinging a foot, brushing or picking at lint, doodling, pointing the body toward an exit, or looking at one's watch or at the exit.

In addition to observing gesture clusters, be watchful for changes in the gestures themselves, which can indicate important changes in attitudes. For example:

Positive Change ↔	Negative Change
Relaxing	Tensing
Increased eye contact	Decreased eye contact
Leaning forward	Leaning away
Uncrossing arms, legs	Crossing arms, legs
Matching body position and gestures with other person's	Fidgeting
Smiling	Frowning

Listen for changes in vocal intonation   Your total reception of a customer's message depends not only on the verbal and visual aspects of communication, but also on what you hear *behind* the words—the *vocal* part of the message heard through voice intonations.

People can project many different emotions simply through their voice intonation. Voice intonation gives the vocal information; the words spoken give the verbal information. Vocal information is that part of the meaning of a message that is lost when speech is written rather than spoken. Changes in voice intonation can help you derive added meaning from the words others speak, and add meaning to the words you speak.

Let's take a look at the seven major vocal qualities that affect voice intonations:

- *Resonance:* The ability of one's voice to fill space; an intensification and enrichment of the voice tone
- *Rhythm:* The flow, pace, and movement of the voice
- *Speed:* How fast or slow the voice is used
- *Pitch:* The tightening or relaxing of the vocal cords—for example, the nervous laugh—and the highness or the lowness of the sound
- *Volume:* The degree of loudness or intensity of the voice
- *Inflection:* The changes in pitch or volume of the voice
- *Clarity:* The crisp articulation and enunciation of the words

The way in which a person varies any or all of these seven vocal qualities in conversation can significantly change the feeling or emotion of the message being sent. A good example of what changes in meaning can result from changes in voice qualities is an actor who verbalizes the word "oh" eight different ways:

1. Exclamation ("Oh! I forgot to mail the check!")
2. Excitement ("Oh! Wow!")
3. Question ("Oh? Is that right?")
4. Passion ("Oh . . . I love opera.")
5. Disgust ("Oh, not peas again!")
6. Pain ("Oh, my arm hurts.")
7. Disbelief ("Oh, yeah?")
8. Boredom ("Oh. How interesting.")

With just simple changes in vocal qualities, a customer can convey eight totally separate and unique feelings and emotions to the salesperson. This simple two-letter word—"oh"— demonstrates the critical importance of vocal intonation in communication.

In summary, sensing is hearing spoken messages through vocal and visual channels. Sensing is very much like learning another language—learning to use and understand *body* talk. As Ralph Waldo Emerson said, "What you ARE is shouting so loud, I can't hear what you are saying."

Step 5: Structure Your Customer's Message to Ensure You Understand

Structuring is listening primarily to the verbal component—the content— of someone's message. The structuring process revolves around three primary activities—indexing, sequencing, and comparing. *Indexing* refers to taking mental or written notes of:

1. The topic or major idea.
2. The key points being discussed.
3. The reasons, subpoints, and/or supporting points.

You can make this process easier by listening for transitional words—words and phrases like, "Well, what I want to talk to you about today is . . ." What follows such phrases is probably the main idea, the subject, or the topic. Also, "first," "second," "third," and "last" are transitional words that usually indicate key points. When people say things like, "For example," or "Let me elaborate on that," you know that a rationale, a subpoint, or a supporting point is likely to follow.

Since we can listen much faster than a person can talk, we can use that time to take notes and make sense of what is being said. You may need to ask permission to take notes; do it as unobtrusively as possible. You don't need to write everything down verbatim . . . just get the highlights to jog your memory later. Taking notes also helps you to focus your attention completely on what your customer is saying.

You have to be able to gather an enormous amount of information, make sense of it, and find a solution to your customer's problems or a way to help her meet her goals . . . ideally through using your product or service. In order to gather and organize all that information, you can use an advanced note-taking technique called *mind mapping* that also helps you find creative solutions to the customer's problems. This technique helps you take notes quickly without breaking the flow of the conversation and helps you to create on paper a visual of what your customer is saying. It is a superior note-taking method in five important ways.

1. It increases the speed with which you can structure and organize the content of what you hear.
2. It increases your comprehension and helps you to recall the conversation when you refer to your notes afterward.
3. It motivates you to keep pace with the customer.
4. It can help get your client involved with the process of information gathering.

5. It lets your client appreciate your efforts to make sense of his situation and help him find solutions.

Mind mapping sounds complex, but it's actually quite simple. Because it looks different from most note-taking systems, it also helps differentiate you from your competition. Because we can think four times as fast as a customer can talk, our thoughts often race ahead of the customer, and we detach from what is being said. Through mind mapping, you can easily remain focused on the customer. It's extremely easy to use. Here are the basics:

- *Focus:* Print the central or main idea in a circle or box in the center of your page.
- *Branches:* Write the key ideas or thoughts expressed on lines (branches) connected to the center focus.
- *Twigs:* Draw sub-branches or twigs—one for each related idea expressed, and connect the twigs to the key idea each supports.
- *Key words:* Write key words only. Mind mapping is a form of brain shorthand and requires only key words to jog your memory.
- *Symbols/Images:* Use any symbols or images that make sense to you. Make use of arrows, pictures, or other symbols meaningful to you—whatever jogs your memory and doesn't take your mind off what you're hearing.

Mind mapping is fun, it doesn't intrude on your concentration, and it captures the essence of what you are listening for. There are two ways you can use mind mapping with your customers. You can just develop a mind map informally as you ask the customer questions, or you can actually prepare in advance a mind map of the information you want to gather from the customer. This could be on a notepad—something big enough to write on that can be seen easily by both you and the client, but small enough to fit into your briefcase. Start out with your client's name in the center of the page, and then have branches off that for the information you want to gather.

The branches of your mind map will match the topic areas in your list of questions. As you work through the mind map with your client, you'll both have a visual feedback tool that will help you get a complete picture of your customer's needs. You'll also have a guide that reminds you of what information you want to gather. You can make any specific notes you want on the branches. For instance, if you know your customer's industry is facing a potentially devastating series of government regulations, you could have a line off the "Challenges" branch that says, "Govt regs." This will remind you to ask how those regulations will impact him. Or if the prospect is in the highest tax bracket, you could devote a branch to that to explore how it might affect his estate planning or pension needs. Figure 8.1 is an example of a mind map.

One of the things mind mapping does is give both of you an overview of the situation. It keeps you from getting bogged down in details. And it also encourages your customer to complete the picture. The visual representation of his situation will prompt him to keep filling in the blanks until the mind map is complete. It gets the customer involved. It also keeps you involved, so it helps you become a better active listener. Several books are available to help you develop your mind-mapping skills. Check out *Mindmapping: Your Personal Guide to Creativity and Problem-Solving* by Joyce Wycoff or books by Tony Buzan.

Discover the Power of
Listening to Your Customers

You have now learned each step of active listening. The skills are now yours to use . . . or are they? Although these skills are all relatively simple to learn and may appear simple to use, *implementing* them may be a more difficult task, because to do so means breaking through a barrier of poor listening habits that most of us have developed over a lifetime.

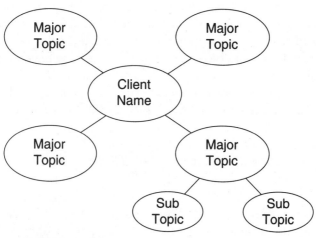

Figure 8.1 **Mind mapping**

Creating and exercising an active listening *attitude* can help you tremendously in breaking through the barrier of your poor listening habits and implementing your newly acquired active listening skills. Exercising an active listening attitude means:

1. *Understanding that listening is as powerful as speech.* What someone says to you is just as critical as what you have to say to them.
2. *Realizing that listening saves time.* People who listen find that it creates fewer mistakes, fewer interpersonal misunderstandings, less employee and customer turnover, and fewer false starts.
3. *Understanding that listening to* everyone *is important and worthwhile.* Approach listening with a new enthusiasm. Look for that something you can learn from each and every person you meet. Focus on the substance and the meaning of the message that people are sending rather than on the mechanics or the style of their delivery.

Summing Up

Listening is obviously a critical part of the exploring stage of sales. We frequently hear salespeople say, "Opening the sales call is the hardest part. I'm O.K. once I get rolling, but those first few minutes are pretty rough. I'm never quite sure what to say." By practicing active listening skills, you make the opening easy. You don't have to worry about what to say or how to say it; you just have to ask questions, listen actively, and follow the direction of the prospect. As you follow the prospect's lead, it is important to stay in sync with him. The next chapter will give you several ideas and techniques for making a powerful connection with your prospects and customers.

CHAPTER 9

Exploring Your Customer's Needs and Opportunities

The most important thing to focus on in the first few minutes of a sales call is getting in sync with the customer. As much as possible you want to match his attitude, demeanor, and business values. Concentrate on his pace. If it is faster or slower than yours, adjust yours. If he is focusing on the task, then get right to business. If he is focusing on the relationship, then take a few minutes to chat. In the first few moments let the client lead and you follow. Wait until the two of you are in sync . . . then you can try to lead the discussion.

Use your competitive advantage statement early in the call. After all, it was the use of this competitive advantage statement on the phone that got you the appointment, so there must be some interest. Remember, your competitive advantage statement should have four components:

1. Your name
2. Your company
3. A statement about a problem in your market
4. How you and your product can solve that problem.

Restating your competitive advantage helps to refresh your prospect's memory and gets the customer grounded in the discussion you are about to have. If he's being task oriented, use it right up front. If he's being relationship oriented, chat for a few moments, and then use your statement as a transition from relationship to task behavior. "Thank you for the coffee. As I mentioned on the phone . . ."

The most powerful aspect of synchronization is *values*. If he believes you share his values, he's very likely to want to do business with you now or sometime in the future. So how do you let the customer know your values are in sync with his? You want to let him know that you are a professional and that you're not just there to make a sale. You want to say something like this:

"My approach to doing business is to partner with you. I am an expert in the products, services, and processes that my company offers, but

129

they will be no good to you unless they fit in your environment. You're the expert in those areas. For us to be effective partners, we have to share our expertise in a collaboration. I'll make you four promises: First, I promise you I'll provide you with fast, high-quality information in my area of expertise. Second, I'll never pressure you to make a decision or to buy anything from me. Third, you have no obligation to buy from me, no matter how much time and effort we spend trying to find solutions. And fourth, I promise not to waste your time. If I don't feel that I can help you, I'll tell you so. You will be in total control of the process.

"In return for my promises, I ask two things of you: total honesty, even when it's something I may not want to hear; and your total participation in the process of exploring your needs and collaborating on possible solutions.

"If you'll collaborate with me, you'll get a free consultant and all the credit for the solutions we identify. I may or may not get an order. The reason I can afford to work with you like this is because you match the profile of my best customers and I want you as a lifetime customer if it's appropriate."

So, once the customer agrees to go along with your "partnering" approach to the sales process, what do you do next? You actually begin exploring the customer's needs and expectations, problems and opportunities, by using your questioning and listening skills. Asking questions is similar to painting a picture. You start with a blank canvas and begin to fill in the background and rough in the picture with broad brush strokes. Then you fill in the details using finer and finer strokes.

Using the "Funnel" Technique of Questioning to Explore Your Customer's Needs

With questioning, start with broad strokes by asking the customer exploring, open-ended questions that fill in a lot about her situation. Questions like "Could you tell me a little bit about your business?" or "Could you tell me what's important to you in choosing a financial institution?" not only start to give you information about your prospect's situation, they give her a chance to relax and tell you what she thinks is important. Open-ended questions do not lead the customer in a specific direction. They increase dialogue by drawing out the customer. If you start with a fact-finding question such as "How much can you afford to spend on a home?" that's an okay question, but affordability may not be your prospect's primary concern right now.

Exploratory, open-ended questions show your interest in the prospect's situation. They often start with words like "Tell me," "how," "who," "what," or "why." For example:

- "How do you see a new computer system fitting into your current operation?"
- "What would you like your new cellular phone to do for you?"
- "What prompted you to look for a new travel agency right now?"

These questions are much more powerful than closed-ended, fact-finding questions that require a simple answer such as yes or no or a specific piece of information.

Of course, we will use closed questions when we need specific answers, such as "How many members of your family will be using the new stereo system?" Closed-ended questions are used to extract simple and specific facts or to direct the conversation in specific directions. But it's important to understand when to use each type of question. Once you've started the questioning process, you want to build on whatever responses you've gotten. You are following the lead of your prospect.

We call this the *funnel technique* of questioning; you start with broad, open questions, such as "Could you tell me a little bit about your long-term financial goals?" You build on the response by then asking narrower and more specific questions. As you move down the funnel, you paint with a finer brush and fill in the details.

Graphically, it would look something like Figure 9.1.

Build on your customer's responses   Assume your prospect responds to your question about why she wants a computer system with "I need more control over our order system." You build on her response by building a question around the operative word in her answer. For instance, you might respond with:

- "What aspects of your order system would you like to have more control over?"
- "What's happening that's making you feel out of control now?"
- "Could you tell me more about your order system?"

When she responds, you'll build your next question around her response to that question, and so on until you feel you've got a good understanding in that area, and then you'll move on to a different area of your mind map and begin again with a broad, open, exploring question in that area.

The broad, open questions at the top of the funnel are comfortable for the customer to answer. They give her the freedom to tell you whatever she wants. By the time you get to the more specific questions, the customer can see where you're going, and she's more willing to share information with you. Not only that, most people experience a higher sense of trust and willingness to share information proportionately to the amount of information they have previously shared. Their willingness tends to increase as they provide more information to you. So knowing how to open your prospect up with comfortable, broad, open questions at the outset of the meeting becomes a significant competitive advantage.

As you move from the broad, open questions to the narrower, more specific ones, you'll develop a clearer idea of the prospect's primary concerns and needs. At the end of the process, you'll probably need to ask more closed-ended questions to get the specific information you need.

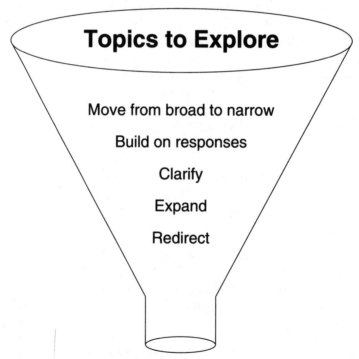

Figure 9.1 **The funnel technique**

Questions are the basis of our information-gathering activities, but it's helpful to understand the three primary directions for questions: expand, clarify, and redirect.

Ask questions that expand the conversation   When you want more information about a certain area, ask an expansion question. You are trying to get a broader picture: "Tell me more about that . . ." "How would that work?" "What would that mean to you?"

Ask questions that clarify   When you are unsure about a given area or are unclear about what the client has said, use a clarification question: "I'm not quite sure I understand . . ." "Can you give me an example?" "What exactly do you mean by that?"

Ask questions that redirect the conversation   When you want to change directions, acknowledge the current issue and then ask a question that brings up a new issue. You are redirecting the conversation to an area not previously discussed: "Okay, I think I understand what you need here; could you tell me how you feel about . . ."

So when you begin questioning, ask your client to tell you a little bit about his business or his personal situation. When he responds, ask him one of the three types of questions. You'll ask him to expand on what he's said and to clarify it if you don't understand it, or you'll redirect him to a new area with one of the other exploring questions on your list.

Whichever questions you use, the purpose of exploring is to uncover and clarify your customer's needs and opportunities. Worksheet 9.1 will help you plan an exploring call with your prospect.

Summarizing and Prioritizing Your Customer's Needs

Once you've used the funnel technique and the direction questions to move through the exploring phase of the sales process, you should summarize and prioritize your customer's needs. Your customer probably has more than one problem or need. If you try to solve all the problems with one gigantic solution, you run the risk of scaring him off and losing everything. The best tack is to prioritize the problems and address them one at a time. Delineate those problems you can help him with, those problems that seem relatively unimportant, and those problems you cannot help him with. Keep in mind that it is always your option to seek other sources to help with those problems you can't solve directly. This prioritization process

WORKSHEET 9.1
Planning to Explore

Write down your responses to the following questions:

1.   What is your objective for this call?

_____

_____

2.   How will you know you've achieved it?

_____

_____

3.   What topics will you discuss with the customer?

_____

_____

_____

_____

4.   List three high-priority, open-ended questions based on the topic categories discussed earlier that you will ask your customer, and three closed-ended questions to use as follow-up.

■ Open-ended: _____

_____

■ Closed-ended: _____

_____

■ Open-ended: _____

_____

■ Closed-ended: _____

_____

■ Open-ended: _____

_____

■ Closed-ended: _____

_____

makes sure that you are addressing first the issues that are of the most concern to your customer. You'll also need to clarify his priorities within each area to be sure that the options you provide fit his success criteria.

The mind map note-taking technique we discussed in Chapter 8 comes in handy here. You can use an asterisk, a check mark, or even a different-color pen to highlight each of the needs that have been identified. If you are selling phone systems, you might say, "Well, according to our map, you're expecting a sharp growth rate over the next five years, so you definitely need a system that's expandable; your customers really depend on your being available, so reliability is a key issue; and most of your employees are not technical, so the system needs to be very easy to use." The key words you've highlighted on your mind map are *expandable, reliability,* and *easy to use.*

If your client has a large number of requirements, just keep highlighting them until the list is complete. Then ask your client to help you rank them. If it's a complex list of criteria and the decision will be made by more than one person, you might want to prepare a matrix including each person's rankings. This would give you a visual indication of the overall importance of each requirement.

When you have finished summarizing and prioritizing your observations, ask your customer if she agrees with your evaluation. If you have been communicating well, there should be no discrepancy. You may want to state this as "Do you agree with my observations of the problems you would like to solve?" On a more positive note, you might say, "Would you agree that these are the opportunities you are seeking?"

Also, *clarify* the customer's priorities within each area to be sure you understand the success criteria against which your options will be judged. Remember, the *success criteria* are those factors by which the customer will judge whether your product or service is successfully meeting her needs.

Summing Up

When you have several different decision makers and influencers, it's not uncommon to find that each may have different—and sometimes contradictory—views of the situation. Prepare a chart including each person's rankings. This provides a visual indication of the overall importance of each success criterion. Once you have their rankings, you're ready to begin collaborating on possible solutions. Step IV provides ideas for making your collaboration sessions more effective.

STEP IV

Collaborating with Your Customer

After you've worked with your client to identify needs and concerns, the next step is to determine whether or not your product or service will solve a problem or expand an opportunity for your client. Usually there are several different ways you can put your product or service together to meet the needs of your client. In the old, traditional method of selling, you would decide what was best for the client and then try to get her to see things your way. The collaborative selling way is much less adversarial and much easier. You actually let the client decide which one of your options makes the most sense for her . . . and then she buys it.

The first step is to collaboratively select the options that look like the best fit. Your client will have as much as or more input into the creation and the selection of options than you do. This process ensures that she will be as committed to implementing the solution as you are. After all, why would she invest her time in creating a solution she doesn't want to buy? After you have jointly identified all the possible options, you can begin to weigh the advantages of each in a joint selection process. Once your client has told you which option best meets her needs, all you have to do is handle the details of completing the sale. What could be easier?

Life being what it is, the sales process generally has a few more twists and turns than that. But if you are acting as your client's guide and are guiding her down a path she wants to be on toward a goal she wants to reach, you will both reach the goal at the same time. And you'll both feel good about getting there! That's the beauty of the collaborative sales process—*everybody wins*. The client gets a solution that solves a problem or opens up a new opportunity, and you make a sale and build a long-term relationship.

The chapters in this section will help you understand how to guide your client through the process of creating options and selecting a final solution.

CHAPTER 10

Creating Options to Meet Your Customer's Needs

If you've done a good job of exploring the needs of your prospective customers, you've gathered more information than you could possibly analyze while you're sitting in front of the client. It's time to head back to your office to begin processing the information you've gathered, formulate some possible solutions, and prepare for your next meeting with the client. Before you leave the client's office, though, set an appointment for a telephone call before your next meeting and an appointment for your next meeting, when the two of you will select the options that will best meet your customer's needs.

At some point in your career, you were probably told that if you're a good salesperson, you'll close the sale on the first call. Now here you are, getting ready to leave, and you haven't even proposed a solution or asked for an order! The selling world today is very different from earlier days when your goal was to get the facts, propose solutions on the spot, and attempt to close all in one call. Today, we face far more complexity in terms of customer needs, the products and services we offer, and the markets we sell in. This usually requires multiple calls.

But with some products, even in collaborative selling, a single contact may still be appropriate. Many companies today provide their salespeople with sophisticated laptop computers and software so that they are able to explore a customer's needs and create and select options all in one call—quite effectively.

This is the case with one of our clients, a major life insurance company. It has equipped its sales agents with highly advanced computerized technology, and this enables them to successfully explore needs and propose highly customized solutions—all in one call! If a company and its sales force have these high-tech selling tools, we're all in favor of a one-call sale. However, unfortunately this is the exception, not the rule.

It's up to you and your customers to determine the appropriate amount of time and the optimum number of calls for your selling situation. Although the focus of this session will be on multicall sales, the ideas are just as applicable, with minor modification and creativity, in single-call sales.

One indicator that it may be time for you to switch from a single-call sale to a multiple-call sale is when you find that you are making a lot of sales presentations but losing those sales to competitors. You may not be as thorough in your single presentation as they are with multiple calls. And remember, a multiple-call design allows more opportunity for you to build the relationship over time.

Propose Multiple Solutions to Your Customer's Problems

When you get back to your office, you'll want to review your sales call and begin analyzing the information you've gathered. Your goal is to create several possible options that will meet your customer's need or solve his problem. Most salespeople make the mistake of proposing only one solution. This is a grave error for two reasons. The first is that you lose the client's involvement in creating the solution. If your client is *involved* in creating the solution with you, he'll be far more committed to its implementation than if you create it without him.

You'll also find that your solution is far more likely to be on target if the client is involved in the *entire* process than if you do part of the process without his involvement. You may be an expert in your field, but your customer is an expert in his business or personal situation. Creating a solution without his involvement *at every step* is a prescription for disaster.

The second reason for proposing more than one solution is that it allows the client to easily see the trade-off of selecting different options. When you present the pros and cons of each option, the client will be able to see that his *ideal* solution may not be possible. That's frequently the case with transactions involving residential real estate, cars, and major purchases, where the desirable options often come at a not-so-desirable price. Giving the client several well-defined options allows him to understand your rationale for making your particular recommendations. It also gives him the flexibility of mixing and matching possible options to come up with the best possible solution available.

Tips on How to Create Solution Options

Try to meet all your customer's success criteria   Review your recommendations in light of what you learned about each topic area you explored, such as timing, budget, decision-making criteria, politics, and so on. Ideally you are looking for a solution that will meet *all* of your client's success criteria. What you'll usually find, however, is that meeting one success criterion means that you may have difficulty meeting another one.

For example, in real estate you may find a great home for your customer that meets her household living requirements, but you may not meet her criteria for quality of the school system or proximity to shopping; or you may be able to meet all the success criteria, including school system and proximity to shopping, but doing so would put her over budget. When you collaborate, the client will be able to help you solve the problem by telling you what is most critical and which factors can be subordinated to others. In other words, if your customer hasn't prioritized her needs already, she'll have to do it now. She may even need to reprioritize in light of the possible options available to meet those needs.

Highlight your competitive advantage   The second thing to keep in mind when creating a solution is that wherever possible you want to create options that highlight those products or features where you have a competitive uniqueness or a competitive advantage. By designing your options and recommendations around your competitive strengths, you'll ensure that the competition will have a tough time bidding against you. They won't be able to meet the success criteria as well as you can, since you and your customer designed the criteria together.

Don't hide your company's constraints or limitations   Your third consideration when creating options is *your* company's constraints such as credit policy, deposit required, underwriting requirements, staff burden, delivery schedule, and so on. It's much better to let the customer know these limitations exist up front than to get the order and have to go back later and explain why you can't deliver what you promised. In a recent study, Forum Corporation, a Boston company that provides training for salespeople and sales managers, found that clients value *reliability* much more than responsiveness. In other words, it's better to promise a little and deliver what you promise than to promise a lot and then not be able to deliver it.

Collaborating on Flexible Products Versus Fixed Products

Flexible products and fixed products require different methods of creating solutions. A good example of a *flexible* product might be a computer. You can create an almost completely custom computer from off-the-shelf components. You can add memory, a fax modem, a bigger or smaller screen, different types of keyboards, a mouse, and thousands of software programs to solve almost any problem. And if the software you want isn't available, you can write your own, so finding the solution to your computer problem is relatively easy to solve.

But let's say you sell only one line of laptop computers. Only one type of mouse or keyboard configuration may be available, or battery life may be limited by the size of the unit. These are *fixed* or *semifixed* products, meaning you can't change them just because an individual customer wants you to. Selling fixed products can get especially tricky when a competitor offers the feature your customer is asking for.

When selling a fixed product, you'll want to focus on those areas where you have advantages or uniqueness, and if your product excels in areas that are high priorities for the customer, be sure to highlight those. You may also be able to explore further to find out if those features where you have a competitive disadvantage are really something your customer needs or would use a lot.

And don't shortchange your value-added service package. Services like speed of delivery, maintenance, quality assurance books, reputation, training, extended warranties, and financing options can quickly turn a fixed product into a flexible product and make *your solution* the *best solution.*

Describe Your Solution Options in a Report of Findings

When you've figured out which options you'll offer to the client, you're ready to write your *report of findings.* We never write proposals. No matter what you say to customers, they always look at your proposal as the only solution you could come up with. They view your solution as fixed and nonnegotiable. No matter how much exploring you do, you're still sure to miss some details. Discussing the report of findings, however, gives you an opportunity to discover anything you might have missed. Salespeople write proposals, but *consultants write reports.*

In your report of findings we recommend including a section called *possible courses of action.* In your report, outline your understanding of the client's situation and list his success criteria, ranked in order of importance. Then list some possible solutions, including the options the client has to choose from and the pros and cons of each. Last, create a one-page executive summary. When it's complete, you'll be eager to share it with the client . . . but don't mail it!

Meet with Your Client to Discuss Your Solution Options

Remember the phone call you scheduled in your last visit? Always call your client before your next meeting to review what you've come up with and to discuss briefly your rationale for what you're recommending. That way, if you are off target or if something has changed since your last meeting, you'll have time to adjust your report before your next in-person meeting. This is also a good time to get their input as to where they are willing to make trade-offs if necessary.

Never surprise your client with recommendations. Making the mistake of surprising a client—especially in front of his bosses or a committee—can be fatal. Even small surprises, like a change in price, can make him look bad. Be sure to cover all critical areas on the phone. You might ask, "Doesn't that make the meeting unnecessary? If he already knows what the report says, why bother to meet?" You're not going to go over the entire report, just the highlights and the potential problem areas to see if you can get some direction from the client as to the best way to proceed. The reason for the in-person meeting is to go over your report in depth and to discuss each option fully. Remember, this isn't you proposing a solution, but rather you and the client creating and selecting one together. Keep the client involved every step of the way. That's true collaboration.

It's also important to confirm your appointment to go over the report in person. Don't offer to send a copy before the meeting. If the client requests one, simply say that there are a number of things you'll need to go over with him in person, so you think it would be best to just wait for the meeting. And be sure to let him know that while there will be no surprises at the meeting, the two of you need to discuss a number of issues. Worksheet 10.1 will help you assess your product or service in preparation for creating options for your prospects.

WORKSHEET 10.1
Assessing Your Own Products

Write down your responses to the following questions:

1. Think of a customer with whom you have recently completed the exploring phase.

    What is the customer's identified need? _____

    What success criteria will the customer use to evaluate any options presented?

    _____

    _____

    What are your competitive advantages? _____

    _____

    _____

    What are the areas of high customer priority in which your product excels?

    _____

    _____

    What value-added services can you offer? _____

    _____

    _____

2. Identify several options you might offer:

    Option A: _____

    Option B: _____

    Option C: _____

    Option D: _____

3. What constraints (imposed by your company) must you deal with, if any?

    _____

    _____

Summing Up

Once you have presented several options to your prospect, it is very important to help him select the one that makes the most sense for his situation. The next chapter will give you ideas about how to guide the selection process.

CHAPTER 11

Selecting Options with Your Customer

After discussing your report of findings with your client and making any necessary adjustments, you're ready for your meeting to help your client select the solution that most clearly meets her needs. You may be wondering if your client will expect you to present her with a final solution after all the information she shared with you during the exploring phase. Your customer is certainly going to expect you to be prepared, to be able to discuss intelligently the solutions you are presenting, but remember, the customer ultimately wants control over the final selection. She'll want to leave your meeting with a solid rationale for her decision. Remember, too, she may also need to explain her choice to her attorney, her boss, or her team. Your goal in this meeting is to educate the customer and to collaborate with her to find the best possible solution for her situation and to make sure she understands it well enough to explain it.

You'll want to check the degree to which each option addresses your customer's needs and priorities, get feedback on each option, and check the solution against the success criteria you discovered earlier. And remember, you've been telling your client since the beginning that you want to partner with her. *Imposing* a solution doesn't fit the partnering model.

Having the customer work with you to pick the right solution virtually eliminates objections and significantly reduces the need for price negotiation. Perhaps most importantly it makes commitment more likely and more natural for the customer, because she has *ownership* in the solution.

Reviewing the Options You've Created for Your Customer

When you meet with the client in person, start by reviewing the one-page executive summary from your report of findings. *It begins with a statement of the desired outcome* and a brief review of the decision-making and success criteria. Then there's a quick overview of the key options and your recommendation. This provides the client with a "big picture" view of his situation. The overview is followed by the list of options to choose from in selecting the final solution. You will want to review the choices together.

It is often a valuable process to review key assumptions here, such as budgetary limitations or fixed deadlines that are not negotiable. Sometimes those assumptions limit the options you suggest, and it's important for the client to understand the assumptions you are working under. Sometimes clients decide to remove those assumptions in order to expand their options.

You'll want to go from the most important decisions or options to the least important, or go through the decisions in chronological order depending on what makes the most sense in your situation.

Explain to your customer that you need his input on the likely outcomes that would occur if each option were selected. Then walk through each decision point using a technique we call *menuing*.

Menuing: Discussing Each Option on Your List

Show the customer the menu of options and review the key pros and cons of each option. Ask your customer which option he feels would work best in his situation. Remember, there should be no real surprises here because you've already gone over the key decisions on the phone. You should be able to move quickly through most of the menus, but you may find it necessary to stop at one or two for some lengthy discussion.

One of the benefits of this method is that it allows you to discuss the price trade-offs of each of the various options as you go through the report. This helps you in three ways:

1. Your client gets to see the building blocks of the total price, so he has an understanding of where the price came from.
2. Your customer is, in effect, accepting the price for the options he selects as you go along. Clients are generally less likely to balk at the final price if they created it step by step.
3. If a client asks you to lower your price at the end, you can revisit the choices he made and ask him which ones he wants to change to lower the price.

This lets him know that you're not just going to drop the price, you're going to change the solution options as well if he is not willing to pay the price for the optimum solution. Using this method, you'll get full price for whatever choices your client selects.

Many buyers who were trained in the old school will ask a salesperson today if she can negotiate the price. What they are really asking is if you can lower your price. In a true negotiation, you want to *trade* concessions, not just give them away. This method allows the client to see that he can have a completely customized solution, but that he will have to trade off something to get it.

Make Sure You Are *Collaborating* with Your Client

As you present your options, keep the client completely involved. If either one of you is dominating the conversation, you aren't collaborating. Some key questions you should be asking the client throughout the meeting are:

- "What other options do you see that I may not have considered?"
- "What red flags do you see if we were to try to implement this solution?"
- "How do you see this option working in your environment?"

In traditional selling you would be getting objections at this point because you would be *telling* the client what he needed, and he would be objecting to your solutions based on his knowledge of his situation. You would be acting as adversaries. In collaborative selling, you and your customer are *partners* looking for a solution that fits for both of you. You don't get objections; you get a review of needs and objectives. The customer *may* raise concerns about the *appropriateness* of any given option for his situation, and that's fine. That's what the collaboration process is all about.

You need to welcome this feedback as guidance in finding the best solution even if it challenges your view of the situation. It's critical that you try to learn from the client. He does know his company and its people better than you ever will, and he *is* the one paying for the solution. It's your role to help him find one solution that he can be committed to. Remember, it won't be the best possible solution unless the client is *committed* to it.

You want to *encourage* him to shoot holes in your solution and create some options of his own. *Ask questions* that will encourage him to challenge you. When you find that he has a concern in a given area, say, "Let's explore the likelihood of that happening." Or ask, "What impact do you see this having on your organization?"

Help your client relate his concern to the bigger picture and to his desired outcome. You might ask, "Given your ultimate goal of X, how important is Z?" After a full exploration of the issue, including creating some new options, ask him which option seems most workable to him and then move on to the next menu item. At the end of the process of selecting options with the client, ask what else would keep this solution from working. Is there anything else that would stand in the way of its successful implementation? Then discuss with the client what else has to happen to get commitment and implementation. Worksheet 11.1 will help you present and select options with your prospect as well as deal with price trade-offs among the various options.

Keep in Mind Your Long-Term Goal: Your Customer *Relationship*

If you truly can't find a workable solution for your client, you may gain a competitive advantage by walking away. Admitting that you can't find a solution won't *hurt* your image, it will *enhance* it. All of the research shows that a customer would rather have you say up front that you can't help than to try and fail. You promised no pressure and no obligation, and you need to deliver on that promise if you can't solve the problem. You'll gain the competitive advantage of trust and respect, and that's the toughest sale of all to make. Remember that your goal is to make a long-term customer, not a one-shot sale. If together you cannot find a workable solution, walk away for now but keep in touch on an ongoing basis. Needs and goals change over time, and you'll want to be there when the changes occur. With this type of sales and follow-up strategy, you'll eventually get the sale and create a customer for life.

For example, a few years ago, a hot salesman in the computer industry sold 40 million dollars' worth of software in one year. The next year he sold 400 million dollars' worth, and retired with $40 million in commissions at age 37. A significant portion of his business in the second year came as referrals from people whom he had told the previous year that he could not solve their problems with his software.

Summing Up

Trust, *respect*, and *integrity* do pay off in a customer for life who will happily and readily give you repeat orders, referrals, and a reference whenever you need one. And it doesn't take many lifetime customers to build a happy and prosperous sales career.

After you and your client have identified the solution that best meets her needs, finalizing the sale is generally just a matter of completing the paperwork. Sometimes, however, a client will want a formal proposal. The next chapter will help guide you through that process.

WORKSHEET 11.1
Selecting Options

Using your own products and options from Worksheet 10.1, complete this worksheet:

1. Create a menu of options under each key topic area you explored with the customer. Include a price for each option and a total price for your recommended solution.

    _____

    _____

    _____

    _____

    _____

    _____

2. Think through how you will handle any price concerns the customer might present.

    Concern: _____

    Answer: _____

    _____

    _____

    Concern: _____

    Answer: _____

    _____

    _____

CHAPTER 12

Proposing Solutions to Customers

We strongly believe in the concept of *partnering* with your customer by creating and mutually selecting options. But from time to time, you may run across a customer who doesn't want to participate in the collaborative process with you and who just wants you to deliver a standard sales presentation. Of course, the first thing you'll try to do is show her the benefits of the collaborative process from her point of view. But if that approach doesn't work, and if this customer chooses not to collaborate with you, you'll need to revert to a more standard method of proposing solutions. To a collaborative salesperson, even in this situation, the presentation is not a pitch; it is still a give-and-take exchange, a process of taking her ideas and combining them with yours to arrive at a solution that makes sense to both of you. The sales presentation in collaborative selling is not the slick, razzle-dazzle approach that some traditional salespeople use. Instead, it is a well-researched, customized presentation of realistic solutions to the prospect's needs.

Promoting the Unique Features and Benefits of What You Are Selling

The best approach for proposing solutions is to take all the customer's needs and address them one by one, presenting the solutions as you go along. You can spend as much or as little time as appropriate on each area of the presentation depending on the client's needs. Your presentation should cover every issue that could possibly come up. This does not mean you need to discuss every feature with every prospect. On the contrary, you'll cover only those that are relevant. Point out the features and benefits that make your product or service superior by focusing on your competitive strengths.

Your presentation should be clear and well organized. The order in which you present the features and benefits will depend on what you are selling and the priorities of your prospect. With some products, there is a natural or logical order in which to show or discuss the features. In addition, there may be an advantageous place to end. For example, when a realtor shows a house, she knows there is a natural order that most people follow when they tour a home. If you are selling a product that does not dictate a natural order of presentation, use your prospect's priorities as a guide.

Keep in mind the primacy and latency effects. *Primacy* is presenting your big guns first so they'll be remembered. *Latency* is presenting them last. The best combination is to start big; give your most salient features and benefits first. When you give the benefit summary, however, leave one of your best features for last.

Let's talk a little about how you'll handle features and benefits. First, let's define them. A *feature* is some aspect of the whole product that exists regardless of a customer's needs. A *benefit* is the way that feature satisfies a customer's specific need. A benefit is a *feature in action.* Most customers think in terms of benefits. They don't care how it works; they want to know what it will do for them—how it will solve the problems they are having.

Of course, you can always present a feature and its corresponding benefit, and then repeat the process for each feature and benefit, but that tends to bore your customer, and it makes you sound like every other salesperson. We prefer to get the prospect involved by using the *feature/ feedback/benefit* method. Using this approach enables you to get feedback from the customer on the appropriateness of each major feature and benefit your solution can deliver. For example, when discussing the features of a house you might say, "This house has a kidney-shaped swimming pool and a jacuzzi. How important is that to you and your family?" You give the feature and then ask for feedback. This allows your customer to actually create his own benefits for the feature. You'll often find that customers will come up with benefits you would never have come up with on your own.

Here's another example. A realtor was showing a young couple a house. When she pointed out that it had a fireplace, the young woman smiled and said that she had always wanted to have a fireplace she could use as a planter! There is no way the realtor would have come up with that benefit on her own.

If the customer doesn't come up with the benefits you have in mind, you can always point them out. But the benefits they come up with themselves are usually the ones that are most important to them. If they do come up with all the benefits you have in mind, you don't have to say anything. You can just move on to the next feature.

When customers come up with their own benefits, they are confirming the importance of that feature in their own minds and establishing its value. The pattern you follow to review features and benefits will vary, however, depending on the customer's level of knowledge and how technical the options are that you're discussing.

Here's an example that follows the basic pattern of feature/feedback/benefit for a knowledgeable customer, but in this case, you'll start with a statement of the customer's specific problem. You'll then present the feature and ask for feedback. Because the customer is knowledgeable, you'll encourage him to provide the benefit. For example:

> *Salesperson:* I know you've been running out of storage space on your existing computer. [Statement of the problem.]
> This model has a 200-megabyte hard drive. [Feature.]
> Given your current and future requirements, how do you think that capacity will work for you? [Request for feedback.]

> *Customer:* That will give me the storage space I need and then some for quite a while. It sure would be a relief not to have to worry about that anymore. [Benefits.]

Sometimes, your customers have clear needs and priorities, but their technical knowledge is limited. In this type of situation, it may be better to go with the benefit first, followed by the feature, and then request feedback. Here's an example for a customer who has said downtime is costly:

> *Salesperson:* This mainframe has been able to reduce downtime caused by system malfunctions by up to 50 percent over comparable models. [Benefit.] This is because it runs its own self-diagnostics routine every 24 hours. [Feature.]
> Would that downtime savings be significant for your operation? [Request for feedback.]

Your customer doesn't need to be a technical wizard to give feedback on the importance of eliminating downtime, yet this process still keeps him involved.

Whenever possible, encourage the client to come up with his own benefits. If he comes up with important benefits that match your features, he'll be selling himself. Keep these feedback questions in mind to involve prospects in your discussion of the solutions to his problems:

- "How do you see this fitting into your situation?"
- "What other advantages do you see in this?"

- "This is how it fits into your business; how do you see it fitting into your family life?"
- "How do you see this addressing the opportunity we discussed earlier?"
- "How well does this look like it will meet your needs?"

Remember that any feature can have more than one benefit. And any desired benefit can be achieved by more than one feature. When pointing out each, be sure to cover all the relevant possibilities. Complete Worksheet 12.1 for some excellent practice with features, feedback, and benefits.

How to Handle Interruptions During Your Presentation

It's not unusual for the prospect to be interrupted by an employee or a phone call during your presentation. When the prospect hangs up the phone or the employee has left, avoid the temptation to reiterate what you have covered so far. This gives the impression that you are summing up for the end of the presentation. Instead, briefly review the last point you made and then continue the presentation.

If there are too many interruptions, you can point out the situation to your prospect. He might be able to change it. Place the blame on the environment by saying, "It seems pretty hectic around here today. Is there someplace we can go to grab a cup of coffee and finish this?" That may be all he needs to either take you up on your offer or have his secretary hold all calls and interruptions for the next half hour or so. You can then enjoy his undivided attention. If that doesn't work, a last (though perhaps the least desirable) alternative is to offer to reschedule the appointment.

How to Structure a Presentation to a Group of Decision Makers

Here are a few helpful hints you can use when you have to meet with more than one decision maker in a group presentation. Your presentation, depending on the size of the group, may be less flexible than a one-on-one meeting. The larger the group, the more structured your presentation will become. It may not work if everyone jumps in with their feedback and ideas simultaneously, so a semblance of order has to be arranged. Therefore, you'll want to *structure* the presentation; here are some tips.

WORKSHEET 12.1
Features, Feedback, and Benefits

It's very important for you to distinguish between the features and the benefits of your product or service. A feature is built in—it's there whether the customer appreciates it or not. A benefit is the way a specific feature satisfies a specific customer need. When you make this distinction, and learn which *benefits* a customer hopes to achieve, then you won't waste time pointing out features in which that specific customer has little interest. Complete this worksheet for some practice with features, feedback, and benefits.

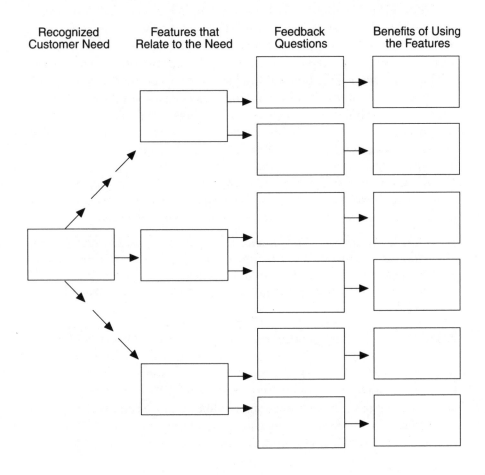

Recognized Customer Need	Features that Relate to the Need	Feedback Questions	Benefits of Using the Features

Provide for a question-and-answer period in the *middle* of your presentation. If you ask for questions at the end and there are none, the silence can be awkward. If someone asks a particularly tough question and you can't answer it or you answer it poorly, you may leave the group with a weak impression. By putting the question-and-answer period in the middle of the session, you can come back strong and finish on a high note. When someone asks a question that is answered in your proposal document, refer her to the appropriate section of the document and assure her that a complete answer is provided. Solicit the impressions of the group. Ask if they agree that the solution you proposed would solve their problem or meet their needs. Don't be afraid to ask questions yourself. The end of your presentation should be like an attorney's closing argument. You'll want to focus their attention on all of the positive highlights of what you've just presented and end with a benefit summary and high energy.

The ideal situation is to have most or all of the decision makers involved during the exploring phase. That way they will have contributed to the success criteria, and the points you discuss will hit on thoughts they have expressed regarding the problems and opportunities at hand. There will be times, however, when you will have to give a presentation to a group of people who were not involved in the previous phases of the sale but who need to hear your proposal to give their blessings to the sale. The following is a general guide for how to structure a group presentation. This type of presentation will be more formal than the one-on-one.

1. Introduce yourself and your proposal   Tell them your name and company and explain in one clear, concise sentence the premise of your proposal. For example, your statement might sound like this:

> "Good morning, I'm Jeff Baxter from International Hospitality Consultants. I'm here to share with you my findings, based on my research of your company and my discussions with Mary Farley, that suggest my company can help you increase your convention bookings by 15 to 30 percent."

2. Provide some background on your company   Give a brief history of your company and its qualifications and credentials. Mention a few companies that you have worked with in the past, especially if they are big names. This serves to "ground" the clients and let them know who you are and the extent of your experience and credibility. Have copies of an account list available for everyone in attendance. Hand out copies either in advance or while you are talking. This list will show them the various sizes, locations, and types of companies you've helped in the past. Succinctly tell the group where your company stands among the competition. Don't get into a detailed analysis of comparative strengths and weaknesses; just make it clear how you compare to your competition by focusing on your competitive uniqueness and advantages. If your company has an impressive money-back guarantee or an extended warranty, mention it.

3. Get the group involved   After you have established the credibility of your company, begin getting the group involved in your presentation. Get everyone's input into the success and decision-making criteria. Preface this with, "I've spoken to Fred, Sally, and Sue and gotten their views on the changes they would like to see in this area, but I'd like to get some input from each of you on this matter." Get each person to add to the list of optimal benefit and decision-making criteria. Take notes, perhaps on a flip chart, on what they say, because it will shape your presentation.

4. Begin your presentation   After everyone has had a chance to speak, proceed exactly as you would in a one-on-one presentation. The primary difference is you want to be sure to answer all the questions, fears, and concerns that arise in the group. Meet each of their specific needs whenever possible.

When you use this method, it is essential during your preparation to brainstorm all the possible concerns and questions the decision makers may come up with. This information will come from talking to people within the company, fellow salespeople, and other people in the industry. You should be so prepared that there is little they could come up with that you haven't already thought of and prepared for. If they do come up with something, you might say, "Let me research that and I'll get back to you." Then make sure you do it!

When you get ready for a group presentation, prepare a notebook with data, specifications, reports, and solutions to specific problems. It should address everything you and your prospect discussed in the exploring phase: problems, success criteria, decision-making criteria, and so on, and how your product or service answers each. At the end of the notebook, include support documents and copies of testimonial letters. *Do not read from the notebook.* It is strictly a resource of facts to give to your prospect after a decision has been made. Do not expect to cover every point unless you can do so relatively briefly. Remember: Documents don't sell products, *people* sell products. Your notebook will in no way serve as a substitute for a first-rate presentation.

The notebook should not contain prices, for several reasons:

- Some people will go directly to the prices without reading through your solution.
- Prices tend to prejudice non–decision makers who should not be concerned with prices.
- Your price may introduce political problems. For example, imagine a group of decision makers who have not had a raise in two years looking at a document that proposes a $2 million expansion plan for the company. You're there to solve problems not create them.

Make it clear that you are not trying to hide the prices and that you would be more than happy to talk about them with anyone they wish; you simply wanted to respect their privacy on what can sometimes be a sensitive issue. As a backup, have copies of the investment summary on hand for each member of the group if they request them.

Ideally, you should find out before the presentation if these people are responsible for dealing with the financial aspects of the purchase. If so, you will have to talk about the costs and the benefits they'll receive in relation to the price. When you give your presentation, address each problem and give specific information about your solution for each one. Make sure you discuss features and benefits and get feedback from the group. Ask things like, "Can you see any other advantages to this?" or "How do you feel about that; do think that would solve the problem?"

5. Summarize your proposed solution   At the end, provide a benefit summary: "Here is what you will get if you accept my proposal . . ." Talk about how the benefits will address the group's specific needs.

Complete Worksheet 12.2 to help you plan and improve a group presentation.

Using Visual or Audio Demonstrations to Enhance Your Presentation

Let's discuss the art of demonstrating. A demonstration, like a photograph, is worth at least a thousand words. Videotapes, slides, audio sound tracks, and live demonstrations are fun, are effective, and keep the pace of the presentation moving. A demonstration aids in learning. By making your points vivid, you make them memorable. Associating new information with images that are already familiar will cement the bond and guarantee the

WORKSHEET 12.2
Creating a Group Presentation

Complete the following form to help you conduct a group presentation.

Standard Presentation Plan

Customer: _____

Presentation focus: _____

Your premise statement: _____

_____

Customer needs you will address: _____

_____

Key benefit you will present after the benefit summary: _____

_____

Where will you use your competitive advantage statement? _____

_____

Group:

Those interviewed (or those who will be): _____

_____

Decision makers who may be at the presentation whom you do not know/ won't have interviewed:

_____

Will the group make a decision during
the presentation?   ____ Yes ____ No

Are they responsible for the financial aspects
of the purchase?   ____ Yes ____ No

Support Document:

Background documents to include: _____

_____

Testimonials to include: _____

_____

impression. Analogies, especially humorous ones, are potent aids to memory.

It is important to make the demonstration relevant. Don't assume the prospect will be able to visualize and appreciate the use of your product or service in her business unless you show her. This is especially true of technical, industrial, and office products.

When setting up a demonstration, be certain all the key decision makers will be present. Produce something of value for them to take home. Give everyone, but especially the user of the product, a chance at hands-on experience. Point out the benefits of its operation. And finally, provide an oral or written summary of the information you want them to retain.

Preparing a Bid with Your Proposal

When you are asked for a sealed bid along with your competitors, it's even more important to learn everything possible about that prospect than if you were going to collaborate with them. There are several things you can do to give your bid more impact.

1. If you can, sell your prospect on letting you write the specifications of the product or service. Nontechnical buyers often look to vendors to help them with the specifications. You should be able to write them in such a way that they will favor your uniquenesses and advantages.
2. Present an extensive comparison of your offerings versus those of your competitors. Be sure you are comparing apples with apples so that your comparison is valid.
3. Meet the specifications and then add something extra—*your competitive advantage.* Describe what your company can do above and beyond the competition. All of you may have a similar product or service, so you have to offer extra benefits such as an extended warranty, specialized customer service, or a different financial package. These offerings can significantly alter the total cost of ownership.
4. Include a list of references so your claims can be corroborated. The key to submitting and winning a sealed bid is to *differentiate your product.* It must have more perceived value while being priced the same as or less than your competitors' product.
5. Finally, include testimonial letters with your bid. These demonstrate the *extra value* of your product or service.

A salesman we know sold football equipment to high schools. His sales included big contracts based on sealed bids. He always included at least three testimonial letters from schools who absolutely loved him. They loved him because he or a member of his staff would always go to their schools' football games and sit on the sidelines with a box full of helmet pads. This was because helmet pads become compressed when a player takes a few hits on the helmet. As the players came off the field, he would change the pads for them. He considered this part of his helmet-supply contract. Coaches liked buying from him because they didn't have to deal with injuries and lawsuits, and he also eliminated the need for them to maintain the helmets and to keep parts on hand. The extra value he added and the letters attesting to it worked wonders for him.

Summing Up

Traditional salespeople often worry about the presentation because they see it as the only time to really "sell" the prospect. Collaborative salespeople don't worry. They know that if they have done their homework and maintained the relationship along the way, collaboration is simply another step in the sales process. The collaboration process is made infinitely easier because they've invested the appropriate amount of time to explore the prospect's situation and are confident that they can propose attractive solutions.

Let's briefly review the steps in collaborating. Remember what we said earlier: If you want to be successful in today's market, you must be able to get the buyer's attention. To do that you must be able to differentiate yourself, your company, and your product. The collaborating phase is the place you do that—where you *really differentiate* yourself from the rest of your competition.

Collaborating begins with the attitude that *you and your customer* are going to work together to create a solution to a problem, or to create more opportunities for *their* business. After you've explored the prospect's needs and concerns, you'll create a *report of findings* that contains multiple options or *possible courses of action*.

Your report becomes the basis of discussion for your next meeting with the customer or for a formal presentation to a number of people involved in the decision-making process. One of the advantages of having a menu of options is that it allows you to discuss price trade-offs as you go through the options.

Throughout this process, you'll be asking open-ended questions, such as "How do you see this option working in your environment?" or "What do you see that I haven't considered?" When you're making a presentation to more than one person, you'll need to address the concerns of everyone present. When they ask a question, ideally you'll be able to refer them to a section of your report that addresses it.

It's very important for you to distinguish between the *features* and the *benefits* of your product or service. A feature is built in . . . it's there whether the client appreciates it or not. A benefit is a benefit only to the client. When you make this distinction and learn which *benefits* a client hopes to achieve, then you won't waste time pointing out features in which they have little interest.

When you demonstrate your product, be sure all the key decision makers are present and that they will each have something of value to take home. (For instance, if you're selling commercial ovens, give each prospect a loaf of bread baked in one of your ovens to take home. That way you'll be involving all of their senses in the decision.) If possible, give the customer a hands-on experience and provide a summary at the end of all the information gained during the demonstration.

And finally, if through collaboration you cannot create a solution that works for your client, acknowledge it. You may gain a competitive advantage by telling the truth and walking away. In today's marketplace, the advantage of integrity cannot be overestimated.

In the next section, we discuss the next phase of collaborative selling, the one many salespeople consider the most difficult part of the sales process—confirming the sale.

STEP V

Confirming the Sale

In this section we're going to discuss some very important points about gaining true commitment from your client . . . how to make *a lifetime customer*, not just a one-shot sale. If you've done your job properly in the first four stages of selling—targeting your market, contacting your prospects, exploring your customer's needs, and collaborating with your customer—your customer should be asking to buy from you! If you've been conscientious throughout the sales process, collaborating closely with your prospect, you should naturally progress to the commitment process *together*. The commitment becomes a *how* and a *when*, not an *if*. So we call this phase *confirming*, not closing, the sale.

A study by Forum Corporation showed that sales superstars seldom use a close at the end of the sale, because they are confirming *throughout* the collaborative sales process. In fact, in 46 percent of their sales, they *never* had to ask for a commitment. It's analogous to asking someone to marry you. If you're unsure of what the answer will be, don't ask; it's probably premature. When collaborative salespeople do ask, it's usually no more than a nudge. Because they are always in step with their customers, the transition from selecting solutions to confirming is natural. Signing the order is just a formality.

Before you confirm the sale, you'll want to be sure your prospect has all the information he needs to increase his perceived value of your product or service. Make sure he understands exactly what he will be getting before, during, and after the sale. Review all of the key benefits you'll be providing and relate each to his success criteria. This summary at the end of the collaboration stage will make the transition to confirming easy. Then simply ask for the commitment using an *open* question that seeks direction, such as, "Where do we go from here?" or "What's our next step?" or "How should we proceed?" This type of question leaves the control of the sales process where it belongs . . . *with the prospect*. No pressure is created. These are straightforward questions that keep your prospect participating in the collaboration process. This method allows your customer to feel that she "bought"—not that she's been "sold."

CHAPTER 13

Dealing with a Prospect's Rejection of Your Proposal

Throughout the sales process, you should always be listening to the questions prospects ask you. These are clues to what they are thinking. The questions salespeople love to hear are the ones that signal an intent to buy:

- "What credit terms do you offer?"
- "Can I try it one more time?"
- "How much lead time do you need?"
- "How does the installation process work?"
- "How soon could training be started?"

When you hear these questions, your response will lead into a natural process of taking care of the sales logistics: order forms, contracts, checks, and so on. If you've developed a good solution and you've established that it's within your customer's price range, the buying commitment should be a natural outcome.

However, sometimes the positive buying questions don't come, and your client starts to back away from the process. There's something wrong—either the prospect isn't giving you complete information or you've missed something along the way. What do you do? This chapter provides some tips on how to confirm the sale, maintain long-term customer relationships, and continually improve your approach to collaborative selling.

Reopen the Lines of Communication with Your Prospect

So, what can you do if your prospect starts to back away? Go back to asking questions! *Candidly ask your prospect what's blocking the decision.* The collaborative sales process isn't designed to put pressure on your customers; it's designed to *solve their problems* or help them to *take advantage of opportunities.* It's what you've done up until now that will make or break the sale. If your customer isn't sold by now, more pressure won't do it. What's needed is more specific communication about what she needs, or what you have to offer. That's why you should ask open-ended questions like, "Where do we go from here?" or "How should we proceed?" and "What do you see as our next step?" You're asking the customer to tell you what else she needs to move the process forward so you can implement the solution you've created *together.*

The sales process we're showing you is a very natural process of two (or more) people sharing information to develop a solution to a problem or need. It requires trust, respect, and open communication on both sides. You can't work as partners through all the stages of the sale and then at the end try to use a manipulative closing technique to clinch the deal. It doesn't make sense.

One of the reasons a traditional close sometimes works is that the constant pressure on the client forces him to tell you what's really holding up the sale. If you can get the same information by communicating openly and honestly, however, there is no need for the pressure. Getting acceptance for a sale means you've done a good job of collaborating. You can go on to *assuring*—the final segment of the sale. But what happens when you don't get an unqualified *yes* at this point?

It's possible that you may have to prod your customer to tell you what's really blocking implementation of the solution you've worked out together. Don't be afraid to ask for open honest communication about what's happening. The client promised honesty and full participation in the beginning, remember?

In traditional selling, the salesperson asks closed-ended questions meant to force the prospect to say yes, such as the forced-choice close, the sharp angle close, or the half-nelson close. The salesperson tries to take complete control of the situation and the customer at precisely the time when the customer most wants her autonomy. She wants the right to make her own decision without being railroaded by the salesperson . . . even if it was the decision she was already going to make. Pressure creates problems in the sales relationship. To reduce the pressure, the prospect may create a smoke screen.

A *smoke screen* is something that obscures the relationship or the decision-making process. Common examples are statements like, "Your price is too high," and "I want to think about it." Both may indicate that your customer is uncomfortable communicating his uncertainty—he's avoiding telling you his true feelings and thoughts. Your customer may also engage in the *objection game*, where she tries to think up more objections than you can possibly overcome. This is a no-win game and a signal that there is a problem with the relationship. A thousand closing techniques won't help you here. They'll only irritate your customer and destroy the trust and respect you've built. And listen to the way it sounds when you say you are going to "close" your customer. How would you like to be "closed"? It sounds like you're terminating your relationship. Instead, you should simply change focus. Using the marriage analogy, the previous stages represent the courtship; confirming is the marriage ceremony. That's the point we're at now. Assuring the results of the sale (which we'll discuss in Chapters 16, 17, and 18) is what we'll do to make sure we stay together long-term.

When you get a yes, you should always review the solution and its benefits, develop a complete implementation schedule, and clarify the customer's expectations and success criteria. This covers things like terms and financing options, payment schedules, delivery schedules, training dates, warranty periods, servicing procedures, and anything else that might not have been covered when the prospect was selecting options. The prospect has now become a customer. You want to welcome him into the family and help him learn how to use his new product or service to his best advantage, and how to get help if something goes wrong. You want him to know that you will be there for him.

Salvage Your Customer Relationship Even If You Lose the Sale

By the time a salesperson gets to the confirming stage using the process we've discussed, there is a high probability that the proposed solution will be accepted. However, there are also some reasons why it might be rejected. We live in a rapidly changing environment—priorities change, people move, people lose their jobs or suffer a sudden loss in the stock market. Companies merge, go out of business, and change directions . . . sometimes overnight. The person who had the authority to purchase your product yesterday may work in a different division tomorrow.

What all this change means is that in some cases, by the time you get to the end of the sales process, you may find that there is no longer a need. In other cases, you may find that you have to start the whole process over again from the beginning. But most of the time, if you've done a good job of exploring, creating, and selecting options, you'll find that things go just as planned, and you'll be settling the details and beginning a new customer relationship.

In those rare cases when you do lose the sale, make sure you don't lose *the relationship with your customer.* If things fall apart at the last minute, you can express your disappointment at not getting to work with the client, and support him as much as you can in whatever decision he makes. Even if he's buying a competitor's solution, offer to give him whatever help you can. The competitor's solution may not work and the customer may come back to you later for help. Let him know that you will be staying in touch.

Use the final minutes of the call to pave the way for the next call, if there is to be one. Note any commitments you made such as price quotes, delivery dates, or terms discussed. Above all, be sure to let the client know that you want to maintain the relationship. Ask him for a postsale analysis of specifically what you could have done better. You will impress him with your seriousness about being able to offer better service.

Evaluate Your Own Performance to Improve Future Sales

If you consistently ask for a postsale analysis, you can begin to catalog the answers and spot trends or problems that you can avoid in future sales. Make notes following each call so you can evaluate your performance. Doing that after confirmed sales will point out your strengths. For lost sales, you will discover your weaknesses by evaluating what transpired, how it affected the outcome, and how it differed from your success pattern. When you get back to your office, be sure to enter the follow-up date in your tickler file, write a thank-you note, and put this customer on your mailing list.

At the end of your day, sit in a quiet place, reflect on the call, and use a *visualization process* to improve your performance. Run the "tape" through in your mind and envision what you did. Then imagine the scene again, but this time see yourself doing everything perfectly. Imagine the prospect's reaction to your new behavior. And remember, it's essential to finish by visualizing a successful outcome. Let go of your mistakes. Trial and error is how all human progress is made. Focus on and hold a picture of yourself successfully completing each sale.

Visualize your successes often. By doing so, you will reinforce the successful and effective things you do. Your mental repetition of productive behaviors will create strong working habits. Use Worksheet 13.1 to develop a commitment plan with a current prospect.

Summing Up

Even if you have performed the sales process perfectly, at some point you are going to experience barriers to the sale in the form of *customer concerns*. We used to call these "objections" and we tried to knock them down, run them over, or trick the prospect into forgetting about them. Now we know that customer concerns are a vital part of the collaborative sales process, and how we handle them determines the strength of our long-term relationship with our customers. The next two chapters will give you important techniques and information for handling customer concerns.

WORKSHEET 13.1
Commitment Plan

Think of an actual customer with whom you are currently collaborating. Complete the following worksheet.

Customer: _____

1.   How are you going to gain commitment?

_____

_____

2.   If you get a yes, what will you say related to:
     Formalizing the agreement? _____

_____

     Implementation? _____

_____

3.   If you get a no, what will you do to:
     Preserve the relationship? _____

_____

     Conduct a postsale analysis? _____

_____

_____

CHAPTER 14

Addressing Customer Concerns

We've talked about what to do if you get a yes or a no from a customer. But sometimes you get a maybe. What do you do if you've asked an open-ended commitment question that seeks direction from the client and he tells you he wants to think about it before he gives you a commitment? You check the five Ps related to customer concerns: price, priority, politics, personality conflicts, and postponement. Let's look at each one in detail: This chapter describes the first four, and *postponement* is covered in detail in Chapter 15.

Clarify the Customer's Concerns About Price

Price always seems to be a major hassle. Theoretically, it should seldom come up because you should have covered budgets, payment schedules, financing options, and so on during the exploring and collaborating stages, but financial and competitive situations can change dramatically overnight. When price is a concern, be sure to clarify what your client means by price.

For example, suppose you're a realtor selling a house for $100,000, and your client tells you that your price is too high. He could be saying that he thinks the house is worth $100,000 but he can only afford to pay $75,000. In this case, you might respond by redirecting the discussion to monthly payments rather than the total purchase price, trying to do some creative financing that would make the house *more affordable,* or finding him a house that's more in his comfort range.

However, when a client says the price is too high, it may have nothing to do with affordability. Instead she may mean that she doesn't really think the house is worth $100,000. In this case she's concerned about the *value* she's getting for her $100,000. We could respond by letting her know of all the special features and upgrades in this house that make it worth the price. She might also mean that compared to other houses she's looked at, she doesn't feel this one is worth $100,000. Here it's important to be sure she's comparing apples with apples, such as quality of the neighborhood, school systems, quality of construction, and so on.

The client could also mean there's someplace else he'd rather spend his $100,000, that this particular house is not worth $100,000 to him. That gets us into *priorities*, which we'll discuss in a minute. He could be saying that he thinks the house is worth $100,000 to someone else, but not to him because it's too far away from his job . . . or he doesn't like the view . . . or whatever. If this is the case, you'll simply add that new information to his selection criteria and find him a house that better fits his needs.

It's also essential to differentiate between price and total cost. *Price* is what you initially pay for a product or service. It's a one-time charge. *Total cost* is what you pay over the term of the ownership, the recurring expenses. Total cost takes into consideration resale value, maintenance costs, performance guarantees, and operating costs. Considerations such as after-sale appreciation, depreciation, or operating costs can significantly alter total cost. For example, with a car phone you pay a *price* for the equipment and the air time. The *total cost,* however, includes the quality of the network and the equipment, customer service and responsiveness, sales support, and other services to enhance the usage of the car phone, such as a voice mailbox, call forwarding, and hands-free usage.

Other price concerns include:

- The size of the down payment.
- How payments match cash flow.
- Interest rates on financing.
- Forms of payment accepted.
- Tax deductibility.
- Other financial considerations.

Sometimes, rather than trying to guess all of the possibilities, it makes sense to just say, "I sense you have a concern about money. In an ideal world, how could we structure the financial package to best meet your needs?" Then work from there to see how close you can come to meeting his financial requirements. Usually, you need only to get reasonably close to get the sale. This is a good way to help the client get at what's bothering him about the financing.

So, obviously, it's important to know what a customer means when he says, "Your price is too high." It's critical to clarify his concern before you respond.

Understand Your Customer's Priorities

The second, and perhaps the most important, P is *priorities*. We've all known a family that had little to eat or wear, yet always had a new car or a new color television set. The same is true in business. If there's one thing we've learned about selling, it's that if your product or service ranks high enough on the priority list, *nothing* will stand in the way of the sale. The mistake many salespeople make is focusing too narrowly when they define their competition. You're competing not just with others in your business, but with any other product your client might buy that would make the money for your product or service unavailable. It's important to establish *your* product at the top of the client's list!

This is where knowing the customer's style, values, and selection criteria comes in:

- Does the customer tend to move *toward* or *away from* particular outcomes?
- Is your customer's primary need for *prestige* or *practicality*?
- How will the customer compare this purchase to other possible investments? By return on investment? Cash flow generated? Payback period? Cost savings? Revenue generated? Budget availability? Political considerations? Personal convenience?

Clients may not even be aware that they are using a particular criterion, so you may have to ask a few questions to determine what it is, but they always have some way of sorting alternatives.

Don't underestimate the power of priority. If you can get your product or service at the top of the list, you can almost guarantee a sale. All of the other P's pale by comparison to the power of priority.

Recognize Problems with Decision-Making Politics

Let's talk about the next P: *politics*. Most salespeople believe they should just stay out of it, and sometimes that's exactly the right thing to do, but typically there are two scenarios you'll have to deal with:

- When *you* or *your product* is the political issue.
- When *your client* or *his project* is bogged down in politics.

If it's your client or his project that's stuck, you'll act only as an advisor. Your primary goal will be to help him come up with some options for gaining internal support. The more options you create for him, the greater the possibilities he'll have for getting it unstuck. Perhaps you can help him to find out what criteria others are using to put their projects ahead of his. Then it's just an issue of priorities.

On the other hand, if you or your product is the political football, the best way to deal with this situation is to head it off in the beginning of the sales process. You should be building support for you and your project right from the start. By finding out who all the players will be and making them active partners in the process, you should have already identified and worked out the politics by the time you get to this point in the sale. If you haven't, you'll need to start at the beginning with these other players, just as if nothing at all had been done. Be completely open and honest with them and dig for their concerns and reservations about the project. Work hard to take their concerns into consideration when you're creating options and selecting solutions. Bring them through the process until everyone agrees to move forward.

A frequent problem with this approach is that your client may not let you speak to the others involved. She may prefer to handle it herself. If this happens to you, ask your client what decision she would make right now if it were solely up to her. If she tells you she would pass on the project, you still have some selling to do with her. You'll need to find out which aspects of the solution aren't working for her and create some new options. If she tells you that she would buy if it were up to her, then ask how you can best help her to sell her project to others.

Politics doesn't just apply to business sales scenarios. They can also arise in a household where a husband and wife or a parent and child are vying for control. One situation we observed was where the husband was ready to write a check for a new "family" car while ignoring the input and concerns of his wife and kids. His wife told him that if he bought the car without taking into account his family's opinions, he could drive it alone. The salesperson was caught in the middle of this political power struggle and couldn't make the sale until it was amicably resolved, fortunately with his subtle and sensitive relationship skills.

Avoid Personality Conflicts with Your Client

The fourth P is *personality* conflicts. This may be the most important concern to handle immediately and well. Your relationship with your customer is the foundation upon which everything else is built. If the relationship collapses, so does everything it supports. This happens because somehow *trust* is broken—your sales style may not be appropriate for the prospect's buying style, or the prospect may not feel that you have a sincere interest in his needs. The way your client learns to trust you is by your doing everything you say you will when you say you'll do it. Each time you don't fulfill a promise, your client trusts you a little less. Each time you do what you promised, your client trusts you a little more.

Another common personality conflict is *no confidence*. The best way to deal with this problem is to never let it happen in the first place. If you're sincerely trying to help your clients, rarely will they lose confidence in you. Listen more than you talk, always monitor how well you're doing with your clients, and always, always, *always* do what you say you're going to do when you say you're going to do it. When problems or glitches arise, make it right. Stay on top of customers' ever-changing needs so you can alter your offerings appropriately.

Whatever causes the personality concern, you need to use all of your communication skills to get the relationship back on track. Assess the prospect's style and make every effort to treat him in a way that matches that style. You might want to review the four behavioral styles—dominant directors, cautious thinkers, interacting socializers, and steady relaters—that were described in Chapter 6.

You may even need to ask during a meeting if there is a personality problem. Here's the way to ask such a direct question: "My philosophy is that if two people want to do business together, the details never stand in the way. Let me ask you this: Given where we are and what we've been through, do you feel comfortable enough with me to want to do business?" If the answer is yes, you can review your prospect's needs to make sure you're both in agreement.

If the answer is no, you'll have to ask the client if he believes it's possible to get your relationship back on track.

- If he says yes, you'll need to pay careful attention to what he's requesting, and be sure to fulfill all his requests.
- If he says no, thank him for his candor and request permission to turn the account over to another salesperson. The best way to do it is to tell the prospect that you want to get someone involved who can better meet his needs.

When you think about the sales process, try picturing yourself and your prospect in a maze together. You're both trying to get to the prize in the center. But you can see only the left side of the maze, and your client can see only the right side. If you lose touch with your customer, neither one of you will get to the center. If you stay together and communicate, you can both see everything, and together you'll reach the center easily.

You're going to try a lot of options before you find the right one, and you'll have to stay with your customer, even if she makes a turn that you think is wrong. Eventually she will realize that she's gone down a blind alley and will start back. To meet your goals both of you need information that the other has. If the customer has a concern, it's because she can see something you can't. You need to find out what she sees so you can start to make progress again. Only through communication and teamwork can you both win.

Offering Evidence to Address Your Customer's Concerns

No matter what method you use to deal with resistance, you must produce evidence to prove what you are saying. That's part of your job. Simply knowing what to say to change a prospect's perspective is not enough. The proof you offer can take many forms.

Make a comparison   Different customers have different buying criteria. If your prospect is mentally comparing your product or service with another, it is essential to help with that process. You can simply list advantages and disadvantages of your product or service versus your competitor's. The method of comparison that you use will depend on what you are selling. The higher the cost, the longer the selling cycle; and the more high tech your industry, the more you will have to use sophisticated comparison techniques. These may include computer data analyses, slide shows, tours of manufacturing plants or other locations, presentations by engineers, and so on.

Present testimonials or case histories   One of the most convincing forms of proof is to present a company that experienced a similar situation and show how your product or service solved their problem.

This can be done with testimonial letters or the presentation of a case history, which can take the form of a slide show. The combination of the two is very powerful.

Present warranties or guarantees   Unconditional guarantees are a very powerful way to make the buying decision safe and easy for your customer. Even conditional guarantees can be very effective. What they say about the product or service is this: "We believe in the quality of what we are selling and have the integrity to stand behind it." Of course, a strong reputation and long history in business help as well.

Worksheet 14.1 will help you compile convincing evidence to address your customer's concerns.

Summing Up

The last P is *postponement* and it's one of the most challenging objections to deal with. The next chapter will give you several ideas for moving from postponement to a sale.

WORKSHEET 14.1
Addressing Your Customer's Concerns

1. List three ways that you can make a convincing comparison between your product or service and that of a competitor.

    a. _____

    b. _____

    c. _____

2. List three companies that can serve as case histories to bolster your presentation.

    a. _____

    b. _____

    c. _____

3. List three people from whom you can get testimonial letters.

    1. _____   Company _____

    2. _____   Company _____

    3. _____   Company _____

4. How effective is your company's warranty or guarantee? List three ways it can be improved.

    _____

    a. _____

    b. _____

    c. _____

CHAPTER 15

Dealing with Postponement

You have been working with a prospect through the sales steps and are confident that you have a solution that meets the client's needs, so you ask an open-ended commitment question and get a maybe instead of the definite yes you expect. Stay calm and review the five P's: price, priority, politics, personality conflicts, and postponement. We discussed the first four in Chapter 14. Now it is time to handle postponement . . . perhaps the trickiest of them all.

We don't like to call the five P's "objections" or even "resistance," because as a collaborative salesperson, you'll encounter resistance only if you're in an *adversarial* environment. If you find yourself in an adversarial environment, the first thing you'll need to do is try to change the environment. To change the environment, just be open with your client about your perception of the environment. Remind your client that you want to be his partner and that you are interested in selling him something only if he really feels it will benefit him and his organization.

When you're in a *collaborative* environment and the relationship is working, you won't get objections or even resistance. But you may get some form of postponement. It's very important to find out the exact reason for the postponement. The client will probably say something like, "I appreciate all your work and it looks like a good solution, but I'll need some time to think it over."

That doesn't tell you much. There could be many motives behind a statement like that, and you'll need to find out the real reason for postponing the commitment. Under postponement we've got four more P's . . . personality style, product, personal comfort, and policy.

Understanding Your Customer's Personality Style

When we say *personality style,* we're referring to directors, thinkers, socializers, and relaters (described in Chapter 6), and this is one area where really understanding the personal style of your customer is important.

181

With *directors* and *socializers*, a delay probably indicates a problem, and you'll need to uncover the reasons for the delay. "I need time to think about it" may seem like a door closing on the sales process, but your ability to ask questions can keep it open.

Good questions for uncovering reasons for a delay are:

- "Which parts of the report are you unclear on?"
- "Which options are confusing you?"
- "It was my understanding that you were working against a deadline—is that still the case?"
- "What specifically can I do that would help you with this process?"
- "Will you be looking at the merits of our solution compared with another, or will you be comparing the priority of this project with other projects in other areas?"
- "Do you already have a source for the cash or will you be looking for one?"

Direct questions like these will keep the door open and the sales process moving along. Let's face it, no matter how much exploring you do, you still may have missed something. Don't just leave your partner there to figure it out by himself. Ask the tough questions that will get the process unstuck.

Cautious thinkers and *steady relaters* are both indirect personality types, which means they proceed slowly and cautiously. They avoid risk and they want to make sure they make the right decision.

Relaters typically need to check with their team before they'll feel comfortable making a decision, so you'll need to encourage the relater to involve others throughout the sales process, not just at the end.

The cautious *thinker* may want to thoroughly review the details of your proposal, or she might need additional data before she can make a decision. The thinker is an interesting style to study because most buyers, at times, act like thinkers. If a major purchase is involved or if a wrong decision could jeopardize their careers, many buyers adopt a cautious, analytical approach to a buying decision. So it's important to know the steps to take with any cautious buyer. Remember that their dominant pattern will be to move away from the things they fear. You'll want to show them that they can solve their problems by moving away from the things they don't want. Here are some tips on how to collaborate with cautious buyers:

Make sure the customer has all the necessary information   If he doesn't, ask what additional information he needs to make a sound decision and offer to gather it for him. Try to stay involved in the process of gathering and evaluating the information. The closer you stay to the process, the more you will be in touch with any changes of direction or additional needs that might be uncovered. Ask the customer to inform you of any change in needs or focus. Remind him that you are partners in this process.

Ask the customer when she will respond to your proposal   Can she identify the date by which her examination of the solution will be complete? Ask if there is a deadline for the decision. Don't push—but do ask. If a decision deadline exists, it gives you a reason to stay in touch and offer additional help or information. Staying in touch during the decision period is critical. If she says her deadline is May 23, ask if you can call her on May 24 if you haven't heard from her first.

Offer to help the customer with anything he needs to get support for his solution   Sometimes this means helping with a presentation to the board, setting up a demonstration, arranging a trial period, or providing a money-back guarantee. Remember, with thinkers it's essential to lower their perception of risk. Sometimes customers just want to do a sanity check. A sanity check occurs when the customer thinks your solution is the right decision but wants to bounce the proposal off two or three other people to make sure he hasn't overlooked any key decision points. It's his last chance to ask, "Am I missing anything?"

Overcoming a Customer's Concern with Your Product

The second postponement P is *product*. If your customer has concerns about your solution, you'll need to explore them. Sometimes he'll tell you straight out that he doesn't think your product will meet his expectations or success criteria. When this happens, you know that something went wrong in the exploration or collaboration stage. Somehow, a high-priority need was not identified during exploring, or you forgot to show how it would be met by your solution when you were selecting options. You'll need to go back to the exploring stage to discover what was missed and then proceed again to the collaboration stage.

When the resistance is due to a technical problem beyond your control, use the compensation method. Acknowledge the deficiency, but try to *compensate* for it by pointing out other features and benefits that outweigh the shortcoming. For example, if you cannot meet a delivery date, suggest other times and emphasize the advantages of another date. This method is effective when the shortcoming is not of paramount importance.

Another option is the *boomerang* method. Think of what a boomerang does. It is thrown out, it makes a wide arc, and it returns to the person who threw it. You can do the same thing when you react to resistance. Imagine a prospect saying, "We are too busy right now to put your product into service." The boomerang response might be, "The fact that you're so busy makes saving time all the more important to you. We have already agreed that my product will save you 50 percent of the time you are currently spending. If you invest a little time now to install it, you will find yourself with more time at the end of the month than you expected."

As an alternative, try changing the premise. In this case, you take the premise on which the prospect is basing her response and change it so she can see it in a different light. For example, the prospect says: "This won't accomplish the XYZ process." Your response could be, "When we first spoke you said you liked our product because of its convenience. We then discussed the fact that it might also accomplish the XYZ process as a secondary benefit. Is convenience still your number-one priority? If not, how would you rate the relative importance of each priority now?"

Assess Your Client's Level of Personal Comfort

The third postponement P is *personal comfort*. These concerns are often the toughest to diagnose. Your client may tell you that he isn't really sure what the problem is; he just wants to think about it. He is probably concerned about the *risk* involved. Try to find out how your client is perceiving the risk of your solution. One good technique is to have him list the pros and cons from his point of view. There are several ways you can reduce a customer's perception of risk:

Guarantee your product   If you offer a money-back guarantee, now is the time to reinforce that message and talk about the specifics of how it works.

Provide evidence of success in other companies   Perhaps your solution is based on a new technology that management has been resisting. You might be able to take the customer to see a successful implementation in another company or talk to one of your other customers on the phone.

Set up a pilot project   You might offer a pilot project to let your customer *sample* your product or service in a limited way before proceeding with the entire project. A pilot is where your customer commits to the entire project but rolls it out only one stage at a time. (A stage might be one location, one new computer, one plant, whatever.) After reviewing the results, she would then roll out the whole project as is, make changes, or cancel the balance of the contract. A small pilot project allows you to prove to your customer that everything you have said about your product and service is true.

How you handle *payment* in a pilot can be critical. If your customer doesn't have to commit and pay up front, he will be more likely to look for holes in the solution because if it works he'll have to write a big check. He will also be more likely to view it as *your* solution and not *his* solution. Therefore, ask the client to commit to the project and place the *entire order* with the stipulation that if the pilot doesn't go well, he can cancel and get a full refund for the unused portion of his order. Once he's made the financial commitment, your client and others in his company will work hard to ensure that what they've already committed to works out.

Help your client analyze the competition—to your advantage   If your client insists on shopping around before she'll commit, make her a better shopper! Assuming that you've done your job and that you have a good solution, you'll want to make sure that she is at least as demanding of other potential vendors as she has been of you. Help her identify the key factors she should take into account, and help her develop a list of questions to ask. Explain the significance of each question to her situation.

Provide information on your competitors, including strengths and weaknesses. This is an excellent opportunity to highlight your *competitive advantages* and *uniqueness*. Volunteer to serve as a consultant or a sounding board, answering any questions that come up as the customer shops. Help the customer compare and evaluate the other solutions gathered. Ask for her commitment to discuss the findings with you when she's through shopping but *before* she's made a final decision.

Overcoming Problems with Company Policy

The fourth postponement P is *policy*. You should handle it almost the same way that you handle the customer who wants to shop around. Occasionally, you'll run into a customer who really wants to buy your solution, but his company has a policy that requires getting three bids for everything purchased. Help write the specs if you can, and then do everything else just as you would for the shopper.

Getting a Psychological Commitment from Your Client

Sometimes you'll find that even though your customer likes your solution, he just wants to make sure there isn't something better out there. Maybe you're the first salesperson he's talked to. If this is the case, it's often effective to offer a tentative confirmation. The customer commits to buy your product but reserves the right to cancel under certain specified conditions. Many travel agents use this method; even though a customer is not bound, he's made a psychological commitment to take the trip. That psychological commitment stops the shopping process, and your customer will have a higher comfort level knowing that he can cancel if he decides to.

An example of psychological commitment occurred when a neighbor wanted to have a pool built in his backyard. The pool salesperson gave him a really good proposal. He liked it a lot, but he didn't feel comfortable signing the contract without checking around. The salesperson told his client that it would take 15 days to get the necessary permits and offered to go ahead with the permits if the client would sign the agreement. This allowed our neighbor, the client, time to shop around during those 15 days and cancel if he found something better. He signed the agreement and never did get around to doing the comparison shopping!

Many salespeople are very flexible about what they allow the prospect to write into the contract. Clients may say they want to check with certain people and that any one of them can have veto power, or that if they can get a lower bid they can cancel without penalty within a certain period of time. Experienced salespeople don't worry about it because they know the prospects are just getting comfortable with their investment decision and covering their downside risk. Usually within a few days, they've forgotten all about their concerns and are working hard to make sure that the solution they created is implemented in the best possible way.

How to Find Out the Reason for Postponement

There may be times when you are unclear about exactly what's causing the postponement. If you find yourself in this situation, you can always use this simple four-step process: *listen, clarify, resolve, and confirm.*

1. *Listen:* Hear the customer out. Listen carefully for clues as to the real concern. Remember that you need to hear the complete concern before you can respond.
2. *Clarify:* Question to make sure you have a complete understanding of the concern from the customer's point of view. What does she mean when she says she isn't sure your product or service will meet her needs, or she's not sure it will work in her environment?
3. Then move to *resolve:* Respond appropriately to the concern. Your response will obviously vary depending on whether the concern is price, priority, politics, personality conflicts, or postponement.
4. Finally, *confirm:* Make sure that your solution did resolve her concern. The worst mistake you can make is to move on thinking you've solved a problem that still exists.

Another great method for resolving customer concerns is to *develop a script.* This is a set of detailed responses to common customer concerns that each salesperson develops for her product and company. One way to develop a powerful script is to have all the salespeople meet and come up with the customer concerns they encounter most frequently. These concerns are discussed one at a time, with each salesperson describing his or her most effective response. The responses that seem most useful to each salesperson can be added to their personal scripts.

When you discover many concerns expressed repeatedly, find ways to preempt them during the presentation. Top salespeople build the answers or responses to these common concerns into the sales process before the client ever brings them up. This eliminates the concern before it becomes significant to the prospect. But you can't cover all concerns in advance, or else the sales presentation would go on forever and be boring to the faster-paced prospects. So you need to have strong, well-thought-out responses to all possible customer concerns.

A blunt statement is difficult to respond to. You can, however, convert the statement to a question and answer it. For example, if your customer says, "I don't think I could use that product," you could respond, "What I hear you wondering is, what benefits would this product bring you?" You can then proceed to answer the question, not rebut the statement.

Summing Up

Integrity in business is essential, and it dictates, among other things, that you work toward win-win solutions with everyone. Managing resistance is simply using different forms of logic to help you be a better consultant. There will be times when your prospect does not see her problems or the solution to her problems clearly. It is your job to gently and diplomatically return with her to a point of agreement and begin again from there.

Dealing with a customer's postponement is a major part of the sales process. Although postponement is a challenge, it's a workable one. Worksheet 15.1 should help you in meeting the challenge.

Once you have successfully worked through the postponement concern and the customer has confirmed the sale, you face your biggest challenge: making sure the customer receives excellent service from your company and from you. We'll deal with techniques for meeting this challenge in the next section on assuring the customer.

WORKSHEET 15.1
Dealing with Customer Postponement

Select a customer with whom you are currently working who has an interest in your product or service but has been postponing giving you a commitment. Answer these questions:

Customer: _____

Company: _____ Industry: _____

1. Describe the current situation: _____

    _____

    _____

2. What reason is she giving you for postponement? _____

    _____

    _____

3. What other factors do you feel might be involved? _____

    _____

    _____

4. Of all the possibilities, which do you believe is keeping her from implementing the solution you've created together?

    _____

    _____

5. Into which of the five P's does the reason she gave you fall? _____

    _____

    _____

6. Which of the five P's do you believe is really the source of the postponement? _____

    _____

7. Given what you now know about how to address the five P's, what will you do to gain commitment from this customer? _____

    _____

STEP VI

Assuring Customer Satisfaction

Step VI in the collaborative selling process is *assuring customer satisfaction*. Even though this step happens after the sale is closed, assuring is the real secret to long-term, extraordinary success in sales. Many salespeople today believe that their job ends when they get the sale. They disappear from the customer's life, leaving service, installation, training, and follow-up to someone else. Unfortunately, they also leave their repeat and referral business to someone else. How well do you assure customer satisfaction? Complete the self-evaluation (Worksheet VI.1) to determine how you rate on customer service.

Making sure your customer is happy with his purchase is the dividing line between good salespeople and the sales superstars. Master salespeople know their success depends on a customer who is delighted the day he buys the product, happy with the purchase decision a week later, completely satisfied with the product and service a year later, and committed to you and your company when it's time to repurchase, whether two years later or ten years down the line. *A customer is a lifetime asset.* The hardest part of the sales relationship is *building the initial trust level.* Master salespeople keep their relationships strong through outstanding *service* and *support.* Their efforts pay dividends through repeat purchases and referrals.

The next chapters will guide you through the process of assuring the satisfaction of your customers. It will give you important tips for servicing your customers, enhancing your customer relationships, and expanding your business opportunities.

WORKSHEET VI.1

Self-Evaluation: How Well Do I Assure Customer Satisfaction?

Evaluate how well you currently assure satisfaction with your customers by completing this form.

	Always	Sometimes	Never
1. I follow up by phone with my customers after gaining commitment.	____	____	____
2. I follow up in person with my customers after gaining commitment.	____	____	____
3. I measure the extent to which the customer's success criteria are being met.	____	____	____
4. When a customer has a problem, I get actively involved in resolving it.	____	____	____
5. No matter what the problem, I resolve it no matter what it takes.	____	____	____
6. After a problem, the relationship is *stronger* than before.	____	____	____
7. I get repeat business from customers who have had problems with my product.	____	____	____
8. I have a system in place to make sure I'm in contact with *all* of my customers on a *regular* basis.	____	____	____
9. My customers feel as important after they buy as before.	____	____	____
10. I measure and quantify the results my customers get from my products.	____	____	____

How do you measure up? If you always do all ten steps, congratulations! You are a super salesperson. If you fall short in some of these areas, however, don't worry. We'll be talking about ways to help you do these things better.

CHAPTER 16

Servicing the Customer

When we are working with our clients' salespeople and we ask them to develop their statement of competitive advantage, they often become frustrated, just as you may have at the beginning of this book. They tell us that they can't claim that their product will cut costs by 20 percent or increase productivity by 10 percent because they've never measured it! If you don't measure the success of your products, services, and solutions, who will? When you do measure, make sure you measure what's really important to your customers. It may not be just quantitative measures. Peace of mind, lower stress levels, closer family ties, and increased enjoyment are all good qualitative measures to monitor. Be sure to measure time periods that are appropriate for your product. For example, insurance agents, stockbrokers, and financial planners wouldn't want to measure dividend performance or investment results on a short-term basis.

You'll find that *measuring results* will provide some significant *advantages* for you:

- It solidifies your relationship with your customers. This is perhaps the most important advantage. If results are good, your customers will be glad to tell everyone inside and outside their company about you. If the results are bad, don't despair. Remember, you and your clients are in this together. You created the solution together, so you'll need to work together to solve any problems that arise. Either way, it's good for the relationship.
- It automatically sets up your next sale. If your results are good, you're in a great position to recommend buying more, upgrading for even better results, or buying another product not yet discussed.
- It helps you quantify your successes. Imagine a year from now being able to say with confidence that your product can cut costs by up to 40 percent! That's a real attention getter, and it's even more compelling when you can present the data to back up your claim.

If you're serious about being a sales professional, you'll need to start documenting your successes today. If you're going to claim to be better, you have to be ready to prove it.

Following Up After the Sale

There is an adage in traditional selling that says, "The sale begins when the customer says no." We believe, however, that the real work of selling starts when the customer says yes. If you'll take the time to determine the lifetime value of just one of your customers, it will help you to understand just how valuable this step is. Stew Leonard, CEO of the world's largest dairy store, believes that every customer who walks through his door is worth $50,000. Automobile companies have placed the value of one loyal customer at $140,000 to $350,000! A 20-year client for a fee-based financial planner can easily be worth over $100,000.

In business-to-business selling, one lifetime customer can mean many millions of dollars in revenue! You have a huge responsibility if you're handling that kind of account. Take a few minutes today to calculate the lifetime value of your accounts. You'll quickly see what it costs to lose just one customer.

At the beginning of the sales process, you have the potential to build a good customer relationship, but after the sale you really have an opportunity to solidify the relationship.

You make *sales* by making *promises* to your prospects. You make *customers* by *delivering* on your promises. You make *lifetime customers* by delivering on those promises *consistently*.

So . . . what does it really take to make sure your customer is happy? First, be absolutely clear on the criteria your customer will use to judge the success of her purchase. You should be thoroughly familiar with her success criteria by the time the sale is made. If not, this is the time to establish those criteria. Simply ask the customer how she would know a year from now whether this had been a good or bad decision. Ask for specific, measurable criteria. Then monitor and measure the degree to which those criteria are being met.

You have to stay in touch. One approach we like to use is the 1–5–15–30 follow-up schedule. We call it that because you'll take specific follow-up action 1, 5, 15, and 30 days after the sale. Of course, this schedule is a guide. Product implementation cycles vary, so adjust your schedule accordingly.

Day 1   Your follow-up starts with a thank-you note immediately after the sale. A short, handwritten note is all that's needed—something simple and sincere, like this: "Dear Mr. Jones, I really enjoyed helping you choose your new telephone system. I trust that it will give you years of service, and I look forward to working closely with you to ensure that it does."

Day 5   The next follow-up, approximately five days after expected delivery of the product, is just to make sure the product has been received and that it's working. This check-up call is especially important to identify any initial problems. For example, if your computer customer hasn't been able to get his favorite software to work on your computer, he may be blaming you, your computer, or your company for a problem that could be remedied in five minutes.

You may find that your customer isn't using your product yet or that he is not using it to its full potential. This should raise an immediate red flag for you. There may be a training or installation problem or it may be nothing, but be aware. Products that aren't being used could kill your future business. When you get this response, be sure to schedule further follow-up.

Day 15   Approximately 15 days after the customer receives the product, call her again. This follow-up lets the customer know you're still available and that you still care about her satisfaction. Above all, it tells your customer that you value your relationship with her even after you've made the sale. By this time, she has received your thank-you note and this is the second call she's received. She should feel well taken care of. If she is still happy with the product, she should be delighted to give you referrals.

Day 30   Approximately 30 days after the sale, send a gift . . . a little something extra. It doesn't have to cost a lot, but it should have a high perceived value and be related to the purchase. For instance, a health club might give new members sweatbands imprinted with the club logo; a computer company might give its customers some public-domain software or a diskette storage box; and a real estate agent might give new homeowners a plant or a nice picture of their new house to share with family and friends.

The gift need not be expensive, and ideally it should be a conversation starter. One of our clients sells car phones and sends customers a pen shaped like the car's antenna. Customers love these unique mementos and keep them on their desks. Others who see these pens pick them up and ask about them. This invariably leads to a conversation about cellular phones, and this frequently leads to more referrals for the salesperson. Worksheet 16.1 will help you develop a follow-up plan for your customers.

WORKSHEET 16.1
Follow-Up Guidelines

Using a system to follow up after the sale will ensure better results with your customers. As you develop your follow-up plan, keep in mind the following techniques:

- Let your customer know about *any* delays in delivery or *any* other problems.
- Confirm that your customer received the product if it is being delivered.
- Check with your customer to ensure that your product meets her success criteria.
- Prevent buyer's remorse by appropriately following through after the sale.

Use the space below to develop a follow-up plan you can use with *your* customers:

Day 1: _____

_____

_____

_____

Day 5: _____

_____

_____

_____

Day 15: _____

_____

_____

Day 30: _____

_____

_____

_____

Be a Customer-Driven Salesperson

Successful salespeople are customer-driven rather than operations-driven (see Table 16.1 for the differences). It is essential to understand the differences in the two orientations. Salespeople focus either on serving the customer primarily, thus being *customer*-driven, or on serving the company primarily, thus being *operations*-driven.

The operations-driven salesperson tends to be focused on *product and business*, always looking for ways to sell the product and make things easier for himself and others within his company. He encourages systems

Table 16.1   The Operations-Driven Business versus the Customer-Driven Business

	Operations-Driven Business	Customer-Driven Business
Orientation	Serves the business	Serves the customer
Focus	Internal	External
	Consistently looks for ways to make things easier for its *employees*	Consistently looks for ways to make things easier for its *customers*
	Creates systems and procedures to protect itself	Sets policies and procedures that are advantageous/friendly to its customers
Sales focus	Product/Feature	Customer/Benefit
Mentality	"How can we sell something?"	"How can we help people?"
Attitude	"If it weren't for all these customers, we could get our job done!"	"If it weren't for our customers, we wouldn't have a job!"
Reaction to an economic downturn	Cut Back Focuses on how to cut costs	Enhance Attempts to create an even greater competitive advantage and uniqueness

and procedures to protect himself and his company. The customer-driven salesperson, on the other hand, is *customer* focused, always looking for ways to make things easier for his customers. He helps create policies and procedures that are "customer-friendly."

The operations-driven mentality is, "How can I *sell* something?" and thus employs a product/feature focus. The customer-driven mentality is, "How can I *help* people?" using instead a customer/benefit focus.

Operations-driven salespeople have their eyes solely *on the bottom line*, trying to maximize profits on each and every transaction, whereas the customer-driven salesperson *keeps his eyes on the customer* and understands the customer's long-term value, thereby maximizing long-term revenues and profits.

In an economic downturn, the customer-driven salesperson survives by creating a *competitive advantage* and uniqueness that makes people want to do business with him. He knows that people will be willing to pay more for goods or services if they are getting more value. In contrast, the operations-driven salesperson is left to focus only on *price*.

Understanding these basic differences between an operations-driven and a customer-driven salesperson is essential if you are going to make a positive change toward being more customer-focused. Complete the questions in Worksheet 16.2 to determine if your business is really customer driven.

The First Step: Show Commitment to Your Customer

What should the *function* of a customer-driven salesperson be? The obvious answer is, "To make money!" Though that may be the obvious answer, it isn't the correct one. Making money is the *goal* of the salesperson, not the function. The function of a customer-driven salesperson should be, as Ted Levitt of the Harvard Business School says, "to acquire and maintain customers." And to be successful in acquiring and maintaining customers requires the first key to strong customer relations—*commitment*.

Commitment to customer-driven service must permeate all of your actions and, ideally, all of the actions of your company:

- Are your actions and the actions of your company focused on doing *whatever it takes* to make your customers happy?
- Are you committed to the *complete satisfaction* of your customers?
- Are new employees in your company quickly and thoroughly *oriented to the customer-driven philosophy*?

WORKSHEET 16.2
Is Your Business Customer-Driven?

Write down your responses to the following questions.

1. What is your company's function in business?

   _____

2. What do you do to maintain a high degree of professionalism?

   a. _____

   b. _____

   c. _____

3. In what industry-related activities do you participate?

   a. _____

   b. _____

   c. _____

4. How do you keep abreast of political, economic, and industry trends?

   _____

   Do you try to think of ways in which they impact your customers?

   _____

5. a. Circle the statement below that most closely describes you:

   (1) "I am committed to giving my customers what they need, even if it means stretching my company's normal operating procedures to accommodate a special request."

   (2) "I try to mold my customer's needs to make things easy for me and my company."

   b. Which statement describes the attitude that your company would prefer that you take? _____

   c. Do a. and b. agree? _____

   d. If no, why? _____

6. Do you have a checklist of things to be done when you receive an order to ensure that product delivery/installation or service commencement is done correctly? _____

WORKSHEET 16.2 (continued)

If you do, what's on that checklist to ensure that things are done right the first time for your customer?

a. _____

b. _____

c. _____

7. Do you work as hard for your customers as you do for your company? _____If yes, in what way(s)?

a. _____

b. _____

c. _____

8. What is your current method for collecting and communicating information to your customers?

_____

Review your description above and evaluate your method of communicating with your customers.

a. Is your method organized? _____

b. Is it done on a regular basis? _____

9. Do you *regularly* check with your customers to uncover new needs or problems?

_____

If yes, define what you mean by "regularly."

_____

10. When you uncover problems with your products or services, do you feed that information back to the right people in your company?

_____

If yes, what results frequently come from your feedback? _____

_____

WORKSHEET 16.2 (continued)

11. Do you engage in joint planning and implementation with your customers? _____

    If yes, what form does it take? _____

    _____

    What is the usual response from your customers? _____

    _____

12. How do you react to customers' complaints? _____

    _____

    From your description above, do you see complaints as (circle one):

    a. Thorns?

    b. Opportunities to improve your product or service or relationship with your customer?

13. Outline below how you would handle the most common complaint from a customer, should a customer call you at this moment with that complaint:

    a. _____

    b. _____

    c. _____

    d. _____

    e. _____

14. Review the responses you have written above. At this point, what seems to be lacking in your customer service?

    a. _____

    b. _____

    c. _____

    d. _____

    e. _____

- Does every employee understand your company's customer-driven philosophy and know *how to implement it* on a day-to-day basis?
- Can every employee in your company explain what his or her job *really* is? Often employees believe their job is strictly typing or delivering or collecting overdue bills; consequently, when they get a call from a customer with an unusual request or a problem, they view it as an interruption of their "job." If, however, every employee in your company knows that their primary function is to get and keep customers, and that every other task in their job description must take second priority, then your business is truly customer-driven.

A company that wants to be truly customer-driven must put everything—its time, money, efforts, words, meetings, slogans, training sessions, and behaviors—behind its commitment to getting and keeping customers. This means that every company employee must do whatever it takes to accomplish that primary function.

Such commitment isn't something that just *you* as a salesperson should feel strongly about, nor is it something that should be felt only by management and the key staff members. Everyone, no matter what their daily tasks involve, must be completely committed to superior customer service. When every member of a company is committed to superior customer service, they know *what exceptional customer service is*, they know *what it looks like to the customer*, and they know *what to do to provide it*.

Key Principles of Customer-Driven Service

Let's look at some of the key principles that help define customer-driven service.

People do not buy things, they buy expectations   You must get as much information as possible about the expectations of your customers. A lot of businesses lose because they believe that a customer buys "things." But, as an example, a customer doesn't simply buy a computer, a *thing* that is nothing more than an electronic box. A customer who is in the market to buy a computer is buying *a solution to certain problems*.

If you deal with customers simply on a level of "things," their evaluations and decisions to buy will be based primarily on price. If customers view the product as a commodity, whether it is or not, they are going to judge it based primarily on price. If, however, customers see your product or service as a *value-added* product, then they will be willing to pay more for it because it is not just a commodity.

Close contact with customers must be maintained   Because you know a lot about your business, you may frequently add products or services without fully understanding your customers' needs—what they want, what they need, and what expectations they have. Gather as much information as possible before you design solutions with your products and services.

By going out into the marketplace and having face-to-face conversations with your customers, you can stay close to them by learning the intimate details about what's really important to them, why they do business with you, what they like and don't like, and what they'll buy and won't buy.

Remember that customers' needs are dynamic, not static. Your customers may come to you for a particular reason, but as things change or their businesses move ahead, their needs change. If you respond only to their initial reason for coming to you and not to their current needs, you may provide them with the wrong solution and lose them as customers.

When two people want to do business together, they will not let the details stand in the way   People want to do business with people they like and trust. When you have a strong relationship with a customer and a problem occurs, his attitude is, "*We* have a problem. How are *we* going to handle it?" But when you and your customer do not have a strong relationship and a problem occurs, his response is, "*You* have a problem. What are *you* going to do about it?"

Creating Moments of Magic . . . or Misery

Every interaction you have with a customer can be described as a *moment of truth*. When an interaction falls short of a customer's expectations, a level of customer dissatisfaction—a *moment of misery*—is created. When an interaction exceeds a customer's expectations, that's a *moment of magic*. Your challenge is to make moments of magic out of as many of your interactions with your customers as possible. If you want to build a base of exceptionally satisfied customers who will go out and speak positively about you and your company and who will literally urge other people to do business with you, you must create consistent moments of magic. When you do, you create demanding customers—those customers whom you have treated so well with your superior service that they are now spoiled. You have raised their level of expectations.

Why create demanding customers? Doesn't that mean more head-aches for you? Think about it for a moment. If your customers know that you will take care of them—spoil them—then they are a lot less likely to go looking elsewhere to do business. This creates severe headaches for your competition, not you, because the competition generally cannot keep up with the high service standards you have set and your customers have become accustomed to receiving. Whenever one of your "demanding" cus-tomers comes in contact with your competitors, the competitors pale by comparison to your company. There are many examples of companies that deliver consistent moments of magic for their customers. Nordstrom's, a retail store, is legendary.

Customer-driven companies attempt to create moments of magic with every interaction they have with every customer.

- They set up systems and procedures to ensure that their customers do not experience problems but in fact experience moments of magic during each and every encounter with their business.
- They develop quality products and services with strong guarantees.
- They hire dedicated employees and train them well, measure their performance, and reward them when they consistently provide superior customer service.
- They design customer-friendly systems and technology.

In other words, customer-driven companies and customer-driven sales-people try to do things right the first time, every time.

But even such customer-driven companies stumble once in a while and create a moment of misery. Complaints arise, problems occur. The way that problem or complaint is handled becomes the moment of truth that turns that misery to magic. The best customer-driven salespeople and companies rise above the rest of the crowd by exerting extra effort to solve the problem *quickly* and assure the customer's satisfaction. Sometimes all it takes is something minor; sometimes it takes something major. But when you can turn a moment of misery into a moment of magic, you take a giant leap ahead in terms of customer satisfaction. Statistics on customer service show that when you resolve a customer problem *quickly*, you create more customer satisfaction than if nothing went wrong at all.

The customer-driven salesperson constantly measures customer sat-isfaction and stays in touch with his customers. Of course, you're opening yourself up to potential problems when you start creating "demanding customers" by talking about measurement, commitments, and expectations. But in today's highly competitive environment, if you're going to survive, you have to have an excellent product and even better service. If you can't meet your customer's expectations, you aren't going to be in business very long.

If you discover that your customer's expectations haven't been met, first look at whether the solution you've chosen is completely unworkable or just needs an adjustment in your customer's implementation plan or perception. Usually, if a customer's expectations aren't being met, the reason falls into one of four categories: *product failure, implementation error, selective perception,* or *buyer's remorse.*

Correcting product failure   Here, something has happened to the product—it isn't working physically or mechanically. The customer will be happy with it as soon as the defect is fixed. But it's critical that you make the correction quickly and cheerfully.

Resolving an implementation or user error   This type of error could be almost anything—sometimes the product is working but the customer doesn't know how to use it or how to use it properly. Thousands of software packages didn't succeed in the marketplace because they were too complicated to use, because their manuals were hard to read, or because the right training wasn't available. It may be an overused term, but *user-friendliness* is a key criterion for success with any product.

Other implementation errors might include your customer not getting along with your trainer or installer, or maybe you've missed a deadline. Most often it is simply the inability of the client to utilize your product or service properly because of lack of training. Many sales involve the installation of a new system or piece of equipment. Naturally, the buyer or the employees must be trained to use it. Given that people tend to forget 75 percent of what they've heard after two days, it is not surprising that user error is a common cause of dissatisfaction after the sale.

Achieving your customer's success criteria will hinge on the effectiveness of the training. It's imperative, therefore, that you *follow through after the training period* to make sure your customer is using the product properly. The more complex a product or service, the better the training must be. Computers are a perfect example. It often takes new computer users weeks or months before they can use their systems quickly, smoothly, and to full capacity.

If user error is a common problem in your business, you should consider training your prospect before you confirm the sale. There are two advantages to this:

1. You reduce user error to practically zero. A well-trained customer will achieve her success criteria immediately or very soon after the sale.
2. Your prospect will be psychologically predisposed to doing business with you based on the time and energy she has already invested in your product. It is unlikely that someone would learn how to use your computer, for example, and then repeat that training to compare it to another. It's just too time-consuming. In addition, to learn the second system she must unlearn yours. That may make it seem like your system is easier to operate. Once your customer is comfortable with her new skills and your equipment, she's much more likely to buy your product.

User error is not limited to the world of high technology. There's an old story about a farmer who went into a hardware store to buy a new saw. He asked the owner for the best one in the store. The owner showed him a beauty and claimed it would cut five cords of wood a day. The farmer bought it and took it home, but returned a week later with it. "I'm sorry," he said to the owner, "but no matter what I do, I can't seem to get more than four cords a day out of this saw." The owner took it from him. "Well, let me see if there's anything wrong with it." He reached down, pulled the starter cord, and the motor roared to life. The farmer jumped back and said, "Wait a minute, what's that noise?" You can never assume people know how to use your product. Take the time to demonstrate it and to train them.

Eliminate the customer's selective perception   This is the process in which a person sees only selected details of the whole picture. For example, your customer may have purchased a new copying machine that works like a charm, but she is irritated by the sound of the motor. She chooses to focus on what is wrong rather than on everything else that is right. Selective perception occurs because buyers expect their purchases to be perfect. Regardless of the purchase price, they figure they deserve perfection. And they do, within reason. When you run across someone who is experiencing selective perception, resolve the problem by pointing out the compensating features and benefits. Paint a brighter picture. Put the negative detail in a different perspective so it becomes an insignificant part of the total picture.

Selective perception can apply to many things:

- Performance characteristics.
- Product operation.
- Product idiosyncrasies.
- Minor inconveniences.
- Downtime.
- The customer's idea about what the solution to a problem should be.

This is well illustrated with one of our client's experiences. Bob Adamy owns a small hardware store near Buffalo, New York. He tells a revealing story about a customer who purchased a Toro tractor. "The customer called me up two years after he bought it. He was ranting and raving because his tractor broke down. I said to him, 'Tell me what you want me to do and I'll do it for you.' The customer demanded his money back. I tried to discuss some other options, but he wouldn't listen. So I wrote a check for the entire amount of the original purchase and told the customer that one of my assistants would deliver the check and pick up the tractor.

"My assistant came back an hour later and asked me to step outside. In the parking lot was my flatbed truck with the customer's tractor on top. Sitting on the tractor was the customer, who had refused to budge. He had the check in his hand. I said, 'I thought you told me you wanted your money back.' He said, 'No, what I really want is to get my tractor fixed. I love this tractor!' So I told him, 'Well, if you just get down, we'll take it off the truck and put it in the shop.' He said, 'No, I'm not getting off this truck. I just want my tractor fixed.' So I got a mechanic, got the parts, fixed the tractor right on the truck, took him home, and got my check back."

Bob's approach to customer service has paid off well. He is now one of the top ten Toro dealers in the country, even though the floor space he has allocated to Toro is relatively small. Bob also has one of the most impressive records for market penetration—a full 5 to 10 percent higher than Toro's penetration in other areas of the country. He is so highly valued by Toro that they asked him to be in their training film with Arnold Palmer.

Overcome the buyer's remorse   Salespeople often underestimate the power of buyer's remorse. Buyer's remorse is the regret someone feels after making a purchase. It can be caused by selective perception, user error, or just an uneasy feeling that he will not realize the full benefits of the product or service. Buyer's remorse could also result from the economic strain the purchase causes. Until he's had more experience with your product, your customer may question whether the benefits will prove to be worth the investment. When a customer either directly or indirectly expresses some regrets in having made the purchase, calm his fears by assuring him that his investment was wise. Repeat the success criteria and the time needed to achieve them. Remind him that employee training and other factors take time to impact performance. If all else fails and you sense your business relationship will suffer, talk to your company about allowing the customer to return the product, if that is an appropriate solution. If your customer is truly unhappy, it's better to give up your commission and still have the goodwill.

Summing Up

The moral of the story is: If you go out of your way to *provide good service* to your customers, they won't make outrageous demands. All they really want is a good return on their investment. In return, they will pay you back repeatedly with *referrals* and *additional purchases*. These customers are truly annuities. If it's not just something simple, you'll have to collaborate with the customer to solve the problem. Find out if their situation has changed, if your assumptions were wrong, or if the product was just a poor match for his needs.

The very worst possibility is that it was just a poor solution to the customer's problem. If you ever want to do business with this customer again, you can't hide. None of us likes to face problems, but studies show that when a customer problem is addressed and fixed promptly, the customer is actually *more loyal* than if the problem had never happened. She's tested your *reliability* and found a supplier she can count on.

Problems give you a chance to show how much you care about the customer. To handle them, you need to immediately *acknowledge the problem* and take responsibility for your part in it. Then you have to do whatever possible to *resolve the problem*. This could be anything from writing a letter of apology to refunding part or all of the cost. Confirm with the customer that your solution was a satisfactory one for him. And whatever you're going to do, *do it quickly*. Speed is essential when a customer has a problem. Too many companies say no, no, no and then, after they have lost all customer goodwill, they say yes. Saying yes up front will go a long way toward building customer loyalty.

If your customer has a major problem, you may need to return to the exploring, collaborating, and commitment stages to find the solution that will best meet your customer's needs. You may also have to make significant concessions in order to keep this customer.

Keep in mind that it generally costs five to seven times as much to win a new customer than to retain an old one . . . and remember the value of just one lifetime customer. There is more at stake here than the profit on one sale; all future sales and all future referrals from this customer depend on your ability to reaffirm your commitment to quality and service. As a professional salesperson, you realize that your customers aren't just part of your career . . . your customers *are* your career. The next chapter will give you ideas for enhancing your customer relationship.

CHAPTER 17

Enhancing the Customer Relationship

After the sale is made, there are two things to keep in mind:

1. *"Out of sight, out of mind."* If your customers don't see you or hear from you frequently, they will forget about you. Conversely, by maintaining regular contact, you will be the first person they think of when they need something new.
2. *"What you don't know can kill future sales."* If you don't know that your customer has taken a new direction or that his company has been acquired, you are probably going to lose this customer.

Two ways to keep up with customer needs are to conduct an annual review with your customers and to maintain constant contact.

Conducting an Annual Review with Your Customers

Let's now focus on the annual customer review. We've found that even salespeople who are good about sending thank-you notes or a gift after the sale usually don't do an annual review. An annual review can be a major part of maintaining your relationship with your customers. A lot can happen in a year . . . people move, get married, have children, change jobs, develop new needs. You have to stay in touch. If the only time you talk to your customer is when you're asking for more money or another commitment, they won't feel that you have their interests at heart. The annual review is a good time to catch up with him and make sure your product is still meeting his needs. You'll often find that your client will ask for your help in areas not discussed previously.

Like any successful meeting, an annual review requires a little planning to be most effective. Here's a quick planning checklist:

- Arrange for the meeting to take place in an area that is quiet and conducive to conversation.
- Take notes and send a clean, typed copy to your client within 24 hours.
- Be organized—have an agenda of what you want to talk about.
- Bring all of the records you'll need to discuss the previous year's business.
- If there are areas where your company fell short of expectations, discuss those first. Outline what steps have been taken to correct the problem. If your company has a quality book, now is a good time to show the client how you'll prevent such problems in the future.

Most important, listen carefully for the customer's stated or implied *needs*, *concerns*, and *opportunities*. This meeting provides a perfect forum for the customer to air grievances, share compliments, and discuss wins and losses. Your actions demonstrate that you are interested in maintaining an open, trusting partnership with your customer. Reinforce this at the end of the annual review by saying something like, "Ms. Jones, I appreciate your insurance business, and I want you to know that I will continue to work hard as your insurance consultant to meet or exceed all of your expectations."

At the end of the review, *offer a new idea, service, product, or promotional deal* when possible. This is an excellent opportunity to spark interest in something new or to thank your client for previous business. Use Worksheet 17.1 to help you effectively complete your annual review with each of your key customers.

Keeping Lines of Communication Open

The annual review is a key way to enhance your relationship with your customer. In addition, as in any relationship, continued open communication is essential. However, anticipate problems whenever possible. You should always be alert to the following warning signs of customer dissatisfaction:

- A decrease in rapport.
- A sudden decrease in orders.
- An increase in complaints—if you're suddenly hearing rumblings about *price, quality, or service,* you'd better act *immediately.*

WORKSHEET 17.1
Annual Account Review Profile

Use the following worksheet with each of your key customers to help you complete an annual review.

Relationship with Customer

1. What is the overall relationship between our company and this customer? _____

    _____

2. How well do we keep this customer informed? _____

    _____

3. Does the customer feel she has access to our key people? _____

4. Does the customer understand our pricing and billing procedures?

    _____

Satisfaction of Customer Needs

5. What are the customer's real needs? _____

    _____

6. How well are we meeting those needs? _____

    _____

Customer's Evaluation of Our Firm

7. What is the customer's evaluation of our knowledge and skill?

    _____

    _____

8. How do we know? _____

    _____

    _____

9. How does the customer describe our company to others? _____

    _____

    _____

WORKSHEET 17.1 (continued)

Evaluation of Our Company in Terms of This Relationship

10. What are the strengths of our company in relationship to this customer?

_____

_____

_____

_____

11. What are the weaknesses of our company in relationship to this customer?

_____

_____

_____

_____

12. How can we minimize our weaknesses and maximize our strengths?

_____

_____

_____

_____

■ A reference to your competition—sometimes you get a clue that the customer is less than completely satisfied with your product or service when he starts to talk about the merits of the competition. He might ask you if you've heard about the upgrade just announced by ABC Corporation.

In addition to these warning signs, sometimes you'll notice a coolness coming from your customer—maybe he doesn't return your calls, or he's too busy to go to lunch. Maybe he doesn't share information as openly as he did previously. His change in behavior may not have anything to do with you or your product, but you'll want to check to be sure. Watch for changes in your customer's personal life, such as a divorce or separation, arrival of a new baby, or death of a parent. These changes can also impact your relationship, especially in the short run.

An event that cannot be overlooked is a change in management or ownership. When a new manager arrives, she wants to make her mark as quickly as possible. She may have loyalties and relationships to other vendors that she wants to bring with her. This is her team. Be sensitive to her needs for comfort and control or you won't be on the new team. It's critical to begin building a new partnership with her. Remember, you are starting over, so begin right at the beginning of the sales process just as if this were your first call on the company. Getting her big-picture view and future orientation is essential.

Another thing to watch for is a big change in sales volume. That could signal a change in the market or in the industry. You need to *be aware of developing trends*—whether they are problems or opportunities—so you can respond to them. Large increases in orders may also signal financial problems. There is no need for alarm, but you may want to alert your accounting department to be sure. Managed properly, this situation could actually work in your favor.

Monitor Your Customer's Ongoing Needs by Keeping in Touch

In the exploring phase, we talked about the difference between the customer's desired situation and current situation. This is called *the need gap*. Our goal during exploring was to have the customer discover for herself how large her need gap was. The larger it was, the greater her desire to take immediate action to close it, ideally by starting to do business with you. It's important not to forget the need gap during the assuring phase of selling. Here, we want to make sure that the customer perceives that her need gap is closed. If so, she'll have little desire to talk to your competitors. But if her need gap is getting larger instead of smaller, especially if it's due to your lack of customer attention during the assuring phase, she's much more likely to respond positively to your competitors' advances, and you stand a good chance of losing the account.

The little things mean a lot in maintaining contact with your customers. Here are some ideas:

- Send interesting articles.
- Introduce your customers to people who might have similar interests professionally or socially.
- Send birthday cards or product anniversary cards.
- Call simply to see how things are going.
- Keep a profile of each customer's interests, likes, and dislikes and keep adding to it. Reviewing it periodically will give you many ideas for keeping in touch.
- Stop by periodically just to check on how your products or services are functioning. Because you see your equipment in a lot of different environments, you may be able to offer tips and suggestions for improving efficiency.
- Talk to others in your company who have regular contact with the client—your technicians, trainers, customer service reps, and the like. They can tell you a lot about how well the product is working for the customer because they work directly with the users inside your client's company. Schedule regular meetings with these people to review your customer's files. Use them as your early warning system to alert you to problems and opportunities. This is one of the best ways to stay in touch with what's happening with your customer.
- Start a newsletter to share new information or ideas from other clients who use the same products. You can also include articles or ads about new products or complimentary products.
- Sponsor user's group meetings so the customer can share ideas with other customers.
- Include your clients in a focus group or quality control board. This is a good way to solidify the partnership with your customer.
- Put together a panel of clients who can help you design your next generation of products.
- When your customer hires new employees, offer to set up a training session for them. Remember, those users will be influencers for the next round of purchases. What better way to make sure they're on your side than to train them from the beginning?
- Encourage your clients to call you at any time with ideas, questions, grievances, jokes, feedback . . . whatever's on their mind. Many top salespeople make it a habit to give customers their home phone numbers. You want to make sure that the lines of communication are always open, and that there is more than one link between your customer's company and yours. The more points of contact

between the two, the stronger the bond. For example, if your customer's head of engineering knows your service technician and feels comfortable calling him directly, it strengthens the relationship between the companies. Think of each relationship as a single strand in a thick cable that connects the two companies. Even if one or two of the lines break, the bond will still be strong and will hold until the broken strands are repaired or replaced.

Summing Up

Enhancing the customer relationship is really just a matter of communicating regularly—listening to the customer's needs, providing him with evidence of your interest, and making sure he has everything he needs to meet his success criteria for your product. Your role as partner is to do everything you can to make your customer successful, because his success is your success. Worksheet 17.2 will aid you in keeping in touch with your customers.

The next chapter will help you understand how to leverage your sales through conscientious application of the six steps of collaborative selling. The results of your efforts pay off in a truly competitive advantage.

WORKSHEET 17.2

Keeping in Touch with Your Customers

Keeping in touch with your customers appropriately is critical to your relationship with them and your success. Use this exercise to identify ways in which you can improve your system of keeping in touch.

1. How would you describe your current method(s) of keeping in touch with your customers?

    _____

    _____

2. Describe the follow-up schedule that you now use after a sale. If you don't have a specific schedule, describe the things that you now do following a sale:

    _____

    _____

3. Think of *all* the possible encounters that your customers and their employees have with your company, e.g., billing, delivery, the customer service department, and so on. List all of the possible encounters below:

    a. _____

    b. _____

    c. _____

    d. _____

4. How can you or your company improve each of these encounters for your customers?

    a. _____

    b. _____

    c. _____

    d. _____

5. Are you now consistently measuring the success of your products or services? _____

    If not, why not? _____

WORKSHEET 17.2 (continued)

Name a recent new customer: _____

What are his success criteria?

a. _____

b. _____

c. _____

d. _____

Are they measurable? _____

If not, rewrite each criterion below in measurable terms:

a. _____

b. _____

c. _____

d. _____

What is a relevant time period for your measurement of these criteria?

_____

How will you relate these measurements to your customer?

_____

_____

6. What are the three most memorable "keep in touch" techniques that have been *used on you* that you can adapt for your customers?

a. _____

b. _____

c. _____

7. What new ideas do you have for keeping in touch with your customers that you would like to try?

a. _____

b. _____

c. _____

d. _____

CHAPTER 18

Expanding Business Opportunities

The customer service techniques in this chapter take some time and effort to implement. Not only are they worth it . . . they're the key to success if you want a career in selling. When you *collaborate with your client* to find the *right solution* and then follow that up with *excellent service*, you establish a strong *partnership* with your customer. That close partnership puts you in the best position to take advantage of new sales opportunities when they arise, and it enables you to expand your customer base inside and outside your customer's organization.

Look for Opportunities to Sell More to Your Current Customers

If you are in your customer's home or company frequently, following up with service or training or just dropping by to talk, you will find clues to new opportunities. These opportunities could be additional products or services your customer needs, or they could be opportunities in other parts of their life or their organization. Complete the self-evaluation in Worksheet 18.1 to determine how well you currently expand your business opportunities.

You should always be thinking *account penetration.*

- Are there any other products or services that would make your customer more successful?
- Could your customer take advantage of discounts by ordering in larger quantities?
- Does your client need a product or service upgrade?
- Look at the total organization—are there other branches or departments that could use your product or service?
- Is the company opening any new branches, stores, or plants in the future?

WORKSHEET 18.1
Expanding Business Opportunities

Complete this form to evaluate how well you currently expand your opportunities with customers.

	Always	Sometimes	Never
1. I follow up with my customers after every sale.	___	___	___
2. I constantly look for opportunities to sell more, to sell a product the customer isn't using, or to upgrade my customers to better products when appropriate.	___	___	___
3. During follow-up contacts, I listen for opportunities to begin new sales cycles.	___	___	___
4. If the customer is satisfied, I ask for referrals.	___	___	___
5. When I am paid a major compliment, I ask for referrals.	___	___	___
6. In asking for referrals, I specify the benefit and source.	___	___	___
7. I gather as much information as possible from the person who gave me the referral.	___	___	___
8. I involve the person making the referral in the process (for example, by asking him to contact the customer first).	___	___	___
9. I contact referrals as soon as possible.	___	___	___
10. I let the person who gave me the referral know the outcome of the contact with the customer.	___	___	___
11. I leverage my current business relationships to create new business relationships.	___	___	___

- Are there sister companies that might be interested?
- In a person-to-person sale, are there other family members or friends who can also benefit from your expertise?

Follow Up on Referrals

If your customer is happy and successful with your product or service, he will generally be willing to help you make connections with others he knows. Ask for his help and then *follow up with the referrals immediately.* And if you do make other sales, make sure you thank your customer and give him some indication of your appreciation. While these gifts don't have to be expensive, they should be thoughtful and appropriate. Flowers and candy are generally safe, but if you know that your customer is a golf enthusiast, for example, a new golf video might be a bigger hit. An invitation to your company's annual golf tournament might be even more impressive.

Intracompany referrals are just like gold. Your customer knows her organization and your product; if she tells you that another department or branch can use your product or service, you have an excellent chance of making a sale. And, because you've been referred by someone within the company, it's like you're family. You have already gotten over the hurdles of fear and distrust.

It's amazing how much gold salespeople leave lying around by not asking for referrals or thinking about account penetration. Every time they neglect an opportunity to ask for referrals, they're taking money out of their pockets and throwing it away. Ask every satisfied customer for referrals within and outside his family and organization. Remember the 1–5-15–30 strategy (described in Chapter 16)? As soon as you are confident that the customer's expectations are being met or exceeded, you should start looking for referrals.

The best time to ask for referrals is whenever you get positive feedback from the customer. For example, if a customer has just told you that she was able to produce a marketing brochure in less than a day using her new color copier, you could ask her if she knows anyone else who might want to be able to produce marketing materials that efficiently. By being specific about the *benefit* mentioned, you help focus your customer. It's a lot more powerful than just asking her if she knows anyone else who might like to have a color copier.

It also helps to get very specific about the *source* of the referrals. For instance, you might say, "That's great to be able to pull a marketing brochure together that quickly. Do you know anyone else in your local advertising association who might need to develop marketing materials that efficiently?" By being specific about the benefit and the source of the referrals, you'll allow your customer to go through her mental list of association members and pull out the names of people who might be interested.

But it's important to get more than a name. Find out what makes your customer think the prospect might be interested:

- What has the referral said to indicate a need?
- What kind of business is he in?
- What type of person is the referral?
- What does he like or dislike?

Find out as much as possible about the referral. This should be done in a casual way, of course. Your customer shouldn't be made to feel that she is revealing confidential information. Be sure to ask permission to use her name when you speak to her referral. If appropriate, ask her if she would be willing to call her associate and set up the appointment for you. If she agrees, it will significantly improve your chances for success.

Contact her referral as soon as possible. And let your customer know the outcome of the contact. If the prospect winds up buying from you, be sure to acknowledge your customer appropriately. If the prospect doesn't buy, you should still send your customer a thank-you note for the referral.

Review Your Customer's Buying Profiles

Always be thinking about how you can leverage your successes. Take advantage of every opportunity. You've worked hard to build and maintain your client relationship; don't be afraid to use it to get into places where you would not be able to otherwise, but be sure not to take advantage of your customers. Leverage includes asking for referrals, but it goes even further. You can further leverage your sales by studying the demographic and psychographic profiles of your present customers to lead you to new prospects who may have similar needs. This leads us full circle back to the targeting step of the sales process!

Which is exactly right—it's a cycle. Each time you make a sale, look at the customer's profile. Analyze his situation and buying criteria. Look at his stage of development, his decision-making process, and who's using which product for which applications. Determine the critical decision points in the sales process with this customer. Then look for other customers who might have similar needs, add them to your list of potential customers, and start contacting them.

Ask for a testimonial or reference   Using your customer's profile to target other prospects is terrific, but leveraging doesn't stop there. You'll want to get a testimonial letter or a reference you can use to influence other potential buyers. Any happy customer is an excellent source for a testimonial letter. The best time to ask for one is when the customer compliments you on what a great job you're doing.

Customers are often willing to give you a letter, but sometimes they'll tell you they don't know how to write one. Tell them it will be helpful if they answer these three questions:

1. What factors were involved in your decision to buy from me rather than someone else?
2. How has my product or service helped you?
3. Would you recommend me to others?

Testimonial letters are evidence of goodwill, and they should be treated as an asset. Photocopy the originals and use them in bids, reports of findings, and your direct mail book. Obviously, you'll need to get permission first from your customer to use her testimonial letter in this fashion.

Make sure you talk to the customer so she knows how often her name might be used and how frequently she might be called upon to discuss your product or service. And, of course, you have to make sure that your customer is always satisfied and happy since potential customers will be calling her.

Summing Up

Your investment in creating a customer who will be your partner will pay off handsomely because he will make it easier for you to sell your next customer. Referrals make it easier because they help break the ice and remove some of the fear and distrust. Testimonials and references make it easier because they reduce the risk involved in the buying process. Substantial leverage is possible when you develop the right relationship with your customers. Complete Worksheet 18.2 to help you expand your business opportunities.

If you make assuring customer satisfaction a regular part of your sales routine and develop a large, loyal customer base, you will, in effect, be *investing in your future* the way people invest in life insurance. Think of each customer as an *annuity*. In the beginning, you establish the relationship. This is like taking out the policy. Over time, you service and maintain the customer, always making sure he or she is satisfied. This is analogous to paying your insurance premiums. As your sales career progresses, you'll find that you have many customers who will give you lots of business. You might consider this the annuity stage, in which your previous investment is paying off.

We use this analogy to give you a long-term view of your sales career and the relationships you'll develop within it. Of course, there's no guarantee that every customer will provide you with income as a low-maintenance annuity would, but each customer you cultivate adds to your income, your referral base, and your reputation as a leader in your field.

WORKSHEET 18.2

Opportunities for Additional Business

Complete the following form to examine opportunities for additional business with your own organization and customers.

1.   What types of opportunities come up most often with your customers?

_____

_____

_____

2.   What can you do to improve your chances of uncovering such opportunities inside the customer's company?

_____

_____

_____

Outside the customer's company?

_____

_____

_____

3.   How can you improve the way you ask your customers for referrals?

_____

_____

_____

4.   What can you do to leverage your relationships with your current customers to help you develop new customers?

_____

_____

_____

Wrap-Up:
Putting It All Together

We hope you feel that we've lived up to our commitment to you to deliver a new kind of sales training book based on *collaboration* and *partnering* with your clients to create long-term relationships. And we hope you've understood that what we've been talking about is not simply some new technique or a new set of sales words. We're describing a fundamental shift in the way you perceive your customer and in the way your customer perceives you. And it all begins with how you perceive yourself. You're changing jobs. You're changing from a person who "sells" things to a person who "consults" and "solves problems" with people to further their businesses or their lives.

To really benefit from this book, you need to change not only your behavior vis-à-vis your customer, *you need to change your perception of yourself in the sales situation.* The first thing you'll need to do is accept the challenge and believe that the principles of collaborative selling work. They *do* work, and soon you'll be putting them to work for yourself. You'll need to develop a plan for how you're going to incorporate these changes into your daily sales routine. Change your habits gradually. If many of the ideas you've heard here are new to you, begin using some of the simpler ones with your existing customers.

If you're already doing a lot of the things we've mentioned, congratulations! We hope you picked up a few ideas that will enable you to have even more success. But let's assume that this approach is somewhat different from the way you've been dealing with your prospective clients.

As we review the principles of collaborative selling, select an imaginary client—one you'd like to become a lifelong customer through use of these concepts.

Step I: Target Your Market

We began with targeting. The most important aspect of targeting is composing your *competitive advantage statement*. Do you have it ready?

Can you quickly state your name, your company, a statement about a problem in your market, and how you and your product or service solve that problem? Can you state what your competitive uniqueness and advantages are, in 30 seconds or less? If you can't, that's where you'll need to start.

Next you'll target your potential customers by *identifying your best current customers.* When you've chosen those you consider best, you look for three things: Who bought what? Exactly how did you find and sell to those customers? Why did they buy what they bought? Having the answers to those questions points the way to where you'll find more customers who fit your "best customer" profile. You'll reach these new prospective customers in a variety of ways: personal advertising, sales promotions, and public relations such as publishing a newsletter or becoming a guest speaker. Or you can generate excellent publicity for yourself by writing in an established magazine or newsletter.

Step II: Contact Your Prospects

After targeting comes contacting. Again, because you want to establish a long-term relationship with this new client, you won't use hit-or-miss tactics or a big scattershot approach. You'll send one letter, then another, then a third. You'll call three to five days after you know the third letter has arrived. Our guidelines here were:

- Mail to four new prospects every day.
- Make your letters look personal and lumpy.
- Always include a headline and a P.S.
- Always include a reply card and a toll-free phone number.
- Computerize your system and *use it every day.*

You'll also use the telephone every day to contact prospects and customers, and in-person cold calls when appropriate. You might go back and review the section on how to handle preappointment objections at this point (see Chapter 5). The most important thing to remember about using any of these contacting approaches is to *be prepared.* Do your homework. *Know your prospective customer's industry* and as much about her current situation as you can. Remember, you're not selling a product or service, you're collaborating with your customer to solve a problem or create an opportunity with what you're selling.

Once you get an appointment and meet your prospective lifelong customer, you'll *determine what her behavioral style is* so you can approach her in a way that's comfortable for her. Review the section on dominant directors, cautious thinkers, interacting socializers, and steady relaters (see Chapter 6). That will help you to identify whether people want a direct or indirect approach from you and whether they want you to be controlling or supporting in your discussion.

Step III: Explore Your Customer's Needs

The next stage—exploring—is where you'll get a chance to get deeply involved with your prospect to determine exactly how your product or service can be of help. It's where the partnering process really begins. You've already done as much homework as possible about this company and its industry in general. Now you'll find out what its specific situation is.

The key to exploring is simple: *Ask open-ended, values-driven, exploring questions.* There are two reasons for this:

1. You want to involve the customer in the whole process.
2. You want to find out as much information as you can in order to provide him an analysis of his situation.

You'll be looking for information on his current situation, his desired situation, and any relevant past experiences that will affect his decision making.

You'll also want to *find out who the actual decision makers are going to be* when the time comes to purchase. You will establish success criteria. And you'll use the success criteria in the assuring stage (Step VI) when you're checking back to see if the solution is really working.

A key skill you'll need to develop in the exploring stage is *active listening.* If you need help here, please review the section on listening (see Chapter 8).

Step IV: Collaborate with Your Customer

After the exploring stage, you'll write a report of findings. It offers a menu of solutions with various options. The collaborating stage begins when you and your prospective customer look together at the options you've created. When you're working with your client to *select options* and *create a solution* you'll keep the client as involved in the process as you are by regularly *asking for feedback* on the options presented. You'll also differentiate between a *feature* that's built into your product and a benefit that will make a difference to your client.

Step V: Confirm the Sale

You'll then confirm the sale because you've followed the collaborative approach we've laid out in this book. Getting a yes for a purchase means you'll move into implementing the solution for your client. If you were to get an unqualified no at this point, you would *maintain the relationship* and ask if you might contact her again in three to six months or when appropriate. You've learned many techniques to help you discover *why* a customer might be raising a particular concern and *how* to address it in the context of a collaborative relationship. We talked about price, priorities, politics, personality, and postponement as temporary obstacles.

Step VI: Assure Customer Satisfaction

You've targeted your customer, contacted him, explored his needs with him, collaborated in developing solutions, confirmed his expectations or handled his concerns, and now he's become a one-time buyer. How will you create a *lifelong* customer? Through the final step—assuring. You'll need to *make sure his success criteria are being met*. Remember our *1–5-15–30 system* for recontacting the customer:

- Send a short note the day you make the sale.
- Call five days after delivery to make sure it's been received and that there aren't any initial problems.
- Fifteen days later, call to ensure that everything is on track.
- Thirty days after the sale, send a small but meaningful gift.

Schedule a review annually, or more often if necessary, to make sure everything is meeting or exceeding the customer's expectations. You'll revisit the exploring stage to see what has changed and what new problems have arisen that you can address.

Building a Lifelong Quality Relationship with Your Customers

Your client has now become a source of possible referrals, and the cycle begins again for you. Targeting, contacting, exploring, collaborating, confirming, and assuring—this cycle is one of the major differences between what we've been calling traditional selling and what we're offering you here in this book.

In the past, sales so often involved a one-shot event . . . sell a product or service and go on to another prospect. Our approach will not only change your style of selling, it will change your life. One of the most common complaints from people in the world of business today is that we don't have enough time for quality relationships. That's a fringe benefit for you as you change your approach. You'll find that you'll develop many new friends along the way.

As you integrate our approach into your selling style, you may find that it feels awkward at first, because it's different from the way you've been selling. As you keep practicing, you'll soon begin to notice that the new way is more comfortable than the old way for you and your customers. Before long, you'll find that the collaborative approach will seem natural to you and you'll begin to forget the way you used to sell.

As you work the collaborative selling system, the system will work for you. Your constant attention to your customers' needs will help you to build your sales career and your competitive advantage.

Thanks for joining us in this sales training book. We wish you the best of luck and success in your career. Actually, you won't need luck; you'll just need persistence. By working the collaborative selling system we've presented in this book, you'll create all the success you'll ever need, because you'll have a *competitive advantage.*

Index